THE CRUMBLING WALLS

BOOKS BY LEWIS S. MUDGE
Published by The Westminster Press

The Crumbling Walls
One Church: Catholic and Reformed
In His Service

THE
CRUMBLING
WALLS

by
Lewis S. Mudge

21 - Prayer
26 "

THE WESTMINSTER PRESS
Philadelphia

ISBN 0–664–24877–2

LIBRARY OF CONGRESS CATALOG CARD NO. 74–101366

BOOK DESIGN BY
DOROTHY ALDEN SMITH

Published by The Westminster Press ®
Philadelphia, Pennsylvania

PRINTED IN THE UNITED STATES OF AMERICA

Contents

Preface

THIS BOOK is an attempt to probe the meaning of certain experimental, radical forms of Christian community life. It is well known that a kind of ecumenical activity has been bursting forth, mainly in the Western world, which alternately scandalizes more conventional churchmen and fills them with hope. This ecumenism is contextual, immediate, unconcerned about, or even contemptuous of, rules and customs made for former days. It is determined to recover meanings that sometimes seem to have flown from the parish church to the life of the streets. While Christian in intention, it is often in intimate contact with movements outside the formally organized church. Walls, which may be intact elsewhere, are crumbling here: between denominations, between church and world, between conventional belief and holy skepticism. Are authentic new structures of Christian faith and life being built out of the ruins?

Leaders of organized ecumenism, Protestant and Roman Catholic alike, began to feel the pressure of these developments several years ago. Among the many and varied reactions at the time was the appointment, by one agency, of a study committee to examine the issue of ostensibly illicit or irregular worship: sacramental celebrations taking place across church lines, or outside of established church structures. The writer found himself director of that project. In the course of the work the focus inevitably broadened. And, with the proper amounts of scholarly procrastination, mature deliberation, and other indescribable processes passing for wisdom, this book happened. It is now presented to the sponsoring body, the Faith and Order Department of the National Council of the Churches of Christ in the U.S.A., as a kind of just deserts. We hope they will like the taste.

At the present moment it is still unclear whether the achievements of a century of ecumenical growth toward unity and renewal are being enhanced, challenged, or largely bypassed by these developments. In any case, this movement toward a new kind of ecumenism cannot be ignored. It has profound implications for the shape of Christianity today, for the relations between Christianity and culture, for man's basic understanding of the meaning of faith. The movement needs to be studied not only theologically but with sociological awareness. In the end, the question is whether there exists, or whether there can be imagined, a social reality capable of articulating in the midst of modern Western culture the kind of transcendence Christian faith represents.

To suppose that these pages even begin to answer that question would be to raise doubts that the difficulties of the question were understood. It is enough if the question begins to be properly posed. The writer has made the deliberate choice of studying a wide range of experimental phenomena, and of being equally catholic in his selection of traditional church forms for comment. This has, for the moment, prevented the further pursuit of a number of lines of sociological and theological argument which may seem promising but which must first be held close to a representative array of empirical data.

Even so, some may wonder if the range of cases studied is representative enough. Most of the examples, experimental and traditional, are Western. This means that one is dealing with situations in which christian (small c) assumptions have played, and continue to play, a considerable role in the culture. One cannot tell for sure how far this fact makes certain viewpoints plausible, certain practices viable, which would look very different if the setting were non-Western. Furthermore, the particular settings of experimentation tend to be ones in which secularization, again in its Western forms, is far advanced: the university and its environs, the metropolis.

In the end, these limitations must simply be accepted, and the study judged for what it does attempt rather than for what it does not. The churches today would have approximately the same set of problems even if the experiments studied in this book did not exist. And the experiments themselves more often illustrate these problems in new forms than offer definitive solutions to them. Perhaps the greatest value of such experimentation is precisely that in it we see the familiar conundrums restated in such a way that the automatic response, the traditional reply, is not quite so easy to offer.

From the beginning it seemed best to expect that the published version of this study would be the work of a single pen. So it has turned out. But the writer owes much to the eminent members of his advisory committee. The original membership of this committee included Sydney Ahlstrom (Yale University), William Barr (Lexington Theological Seminary), Miss Emma Lou Benignus (Episcopal Theological School, Cambridge), Paul Chapman (Packard Manse), Charles von Euw (St. John's Theological Seminary), Boone Porter (General Theological Seminary), John Romanides (Holy Cross Orthodox Theological School), and Richard Shaull (Princeton Theological Seminary). Father Romanides had to withdraw after the first year. John Meyendorff (St. Vladimir's Orthodox Theological Seminary) subsequently read a draft of the section on Orthodoxy, making several suggestions which were gratefully accepted. The committee was shocked and saddened by the premature death of Father von Euw in August, 1969. Father von Euw contributed much to the work of the group, and was working on a critique of the section on Roman Catholicism at the time of his death. Father R. Rousseau, S.J., of the Department of Faith and Order, has kindly checked this part of the book for factual accuracy.

The advisory committee met as a whole three times, and in subcommittees twice. Members contributed historical surveys, case studies, and theological analyses which have been freely used and acknowledged. The writer, however, must accept full responsibility for the present result. Materials not otherwise credited are based on his own research. Viewpoints and opinions are his also: neither the advisory committee nor the National Council of Churches should be blamed for any of these!

A number of other persons deserve thanks for significant help. William Norgren and Richard Johnson, of the Department of Faith and Order, gave constant practical aid. Mr. Johnson had staff responsibility for the study. In addition he prepared a survey of church positions on which the committee freely drew. Georges and Dorothée Casalis, editors of *Christianisme Social,* not only gave permission for the use of extensive materials first published in their journal but checked the writer's translations and interpretations for accuracy. John O. Nelson gave the writer the chance to meet a number of representatives of "underground" churches on a weekend at Kirkridge. John Bartholomew, Thomas E. Bird, Keith Bridston, André Dumas, Daniel Migliore, Daniel O'Hanlon, Ralph Quere, Frank Roseberry, Barbara Troxell, Charles West, Cecil Williams, Colin Williams, and Lukas Vischer suggested ideas and provided leads. Sister Sara Butler and Richard Koenig read drafts and pointed out slips. Martin Conway, formerly Study Secretary of the World Student Christian Federation, provided documents, offered reflections in numerous personal letters and conversations, and most helpfully criticized drafts at every stage of the study. His persistent help and encouragement improved this book in many ways.

Thanks go, too, to the Trustees of Amherst College for the sabbatical year of which this project occupied several months; to the Department of Religion at Princeton University, where the writer spent the year as a Visiting Fellow; and to Princeton Theological Seminary, whose Speer Library provided working space and endless resources. President James I. McCord extended many courtesies and Librarian Charles Willard and his staff were unfailingly helpful.

And, then, thanks to my wife, Jean, who was willing to believe this was important if I did, and who, in the middle of her own writing, took the children swimming while I typed!

L. S. M.

Amherst, Massachusetts

CHAPTER I

Radical Ecumenism:
Dialogue in a New Key

O N JUNE 2, 1968, in an apartment on the rue de
Vaugirard in Paris, sixty-one Protestants and
Roman Catholics, priests, ministers, and laymen, celebrated an extraordinary Communion service together. The
occasion was the uprising of French workers and students
which occurred that tumultuous spring. In the light of
their common pastoral involvement, their bodily sharing in
the issues, the hopes, and the risks of the movement, this
common celebration of the Sacrament seemed the most
natural thing in the world. But a public ecumenical act
like this had not taken place before. Reaction in the
churches was intense. The press was fascinated. Long after
the political scene had shifted, waves of comment on this
breach of church barriers continued to roll in. In a day, the
wall between Protestants and Roman Catholics had developed a visible crack. Hasty efforts were made in some
quarters to repair it, but to no avail. This had been an
earthquake, followed by a tidal wave. The foundations of
the wall were crumbling, the mortar was washed away, the
great stones were left askew. This barrier would never be
the same again.

The Protestant–Roman Catholic Communion service
in Paris on the day of Pentecost was one visible eruption
of a diverse volcanic movement, much of it still unpubli-
cized, which is seething in pockets of discontent and

experiment throughout the Christian church. This ferment
has an ecumenical character, but it is also evidence of deep
dissatisfaction with the ecumenical movement in its organized form. The question, in a word, is whether a half
century of discussion between the churches has produced
any clear examples, any imaginative picture, of what the
community of Christian celebration in the world ought to
be. Is it not, in fact, time to cut through the theological
rhetoric and ask how and where man can worship at all?
What kind of human gathering makes worship possible
and do the churches, as we know them, have something to
do with it? Can the ecumenical movement, organized as at
present, really address itself to such questions or has the
initiative passed to the experimenters, the radicals, who
seek to show the way with bold innovations?

1. THE CRISIS OF ECUMENICAL IMAGINATION

The organized ecumenical movement has impressive
achievements to its credit. In one sense, of course, it has
traded the possibility of rapid progress toward agreement
for greater inclusiveness of participation. On the whole,
the bargain has been a good one. Not only are the great
Eastern churches now fully involved, but the Roman
Catholic Church, if not formally a member of the World
Council of Churches, today makes an immense impact on
ecumenical conversations. But the rather gradual progress
of ecumenism has also carried the movement, its major
problems yet unsolved, into an era of unprecedented theological ferment, and, some would say, disintegration. The
theological comforts associated with the neo-orthodox re-
vival led by Karl Barth have now largely vanished. The
difficulties now faced by the churches in modern society
are more demanding than the ecumenical pioneers could
have imagined. The way forward is in doubt and the out-
come is uncertain. If delay has saved the churches from

being content with easy answers, it has also raised the question of whether, in the places the churches are looking, answers exist.

As one studies the products of ecumenical dialogue, several facts stand out. A degree of consensus has been achieved that transcends many of the old reasons for Christian division. There exists remarkable agreement on the basic outlines of Biblical faith, on the meanings of "church," "ministry," "mission," and so on. Ecumenism has developed considerable inward momentum toward common Christian life and worship, momentum that remains coherent so long as traditional concepts and language are used. A recent World Council of Churches document outlining an ecumenical consensus on the meaning of Holy Communion is a good example.[1] Furthermore, reflection of another sort has produced extremely acute analyses of the state of the modern world, using such concepts as "secularization" and the "end of Christendom." These studies have drawn heavily on the social sciences, and they are conceptually in touch with reflection that is going on outside the organized church. But ecumenical theologizing has not yet succeeded in putting these achievements together in the form of models of what church and faith should be like in the new environment. At least what models there are seem exceptionally difficult to grasp and to put into action. A recent World Council of Churches working paper says this:

> Theologians wrestle with the ways in which new understandings of the corporate and missionary character of the sacrament belong with new commitments to effective worldly action, but their findings have not yet been translated into terms that most Christians can grasp and work out in practice.[2]

The same point has been noted by independent observers. Ecumenically minded theologians, say sociologists Rodney Stark and Charles Y. Glock, think they are presiding over a transformation of the church into new and more effective forms. But nobody can translate their proposals into concrete images.

The subtleties of what is being proposed in place of the old belief seem elusive. . . . The new breed of theologians . . . are telling us . . . that we rigidly identify Christianity with an old-fashioned fundamentalism that modern Christianity has long since discarded. Still, we find it difficult to grasp the substance of their alternatives.[3]

Despite impressive agreements among theologians, in short, we are finding that, in practical terms, our understandings do not work. We sit together in church, bitterly divided about the import of Christian faith for our involvement in social and political questions. We strain to see a real difference, in behavior, character, or otherwise, between "believers" and other men of conscience. What difference does it make to be in the church? Some find deeper fellowship with many kinds of people "outside."

It is time that the theologians listened to the sociologists, for while the latter may lack the training to understand the history and terminology of theological reflection, they are asking what is, in fact, a vital theological question. It is this: Given your recovery of the substance of Biblical faith, and given your sophistication about the modern world, what do you now propose to do? Do you propose to contain the new thinking within the churches as they are at present conceived and organized? Do you not see that new understandings of faith are purely theoretical until they are concretely lived, and that to do this you may need an utterly new *kind* of "church"? Tell us about this: how can we conceive of the new social embodiment of Christianity as you see it?

In his book *The Structure of Scientific Revolutions,*[4] Thomas Kuhn argues that the progress of science in recent centuries has been due largely to the development of models—"universally recognized scientific achievements that for a time provide model problems and solutions to a community of practitioners." But, says Kuhn, it sooner or later becomes apparent that a particular model is no longer adequate for dealing with a limited sphere of reality. When this happens, some people try desperately to save the old structure; others attempt to modify it sufficiently to fit new facts; still others analyze the crisis correctly but have no clue as to a way out of it. The great scientific revolutions have occurred only when someone comes up with a new theoretical framework for dealing with reality that re-defines problems, provides a way for solving them, and thus opens the road to a new stage of scientific development.

It would seem that the present crisis in the life of the church marks a stage of increasing discomfort with the old models of the shape of Christian life in the world, a stage of considerable insight about what the problem is, but a stage prior to the discovery of a genuinely new way of thinking, speaking, and doing Christian truth. We do not yet have the new images we need, the new way of grasping the meaning of Christianity as a living social reality. One suspects, however, that the new models, when they appear, will not be the brilliant discovery of an individual or a research team. Scientific revolutions may happen that way, but revolutions in social insight are more gradual. The breakthrough we seek may emerge more in the way many scientists picture the "discovery" of a "cure" for cancer. The cure may consist not in the application of a single, stunning, insight but in an accumulation of experience with different aspects of the issue, an accumulation that will at some point lead us to realize that we have passed from one era to another. In retrospect, we will be able to see just what the essential change has been.

If anything of this sort is to happen, the analogy just borrowed from the natural sciences suggests that a large input of empirical data is needed. Theories need to be tested against experience. Experience points toward new theories. A way to move beyond the present ecumenical impasse may possibly be found if a way can be devised to make use of the lived-out raw material that ecumenical experiments are providing. That is the purpose of this book.

But not just any experimental material will do. One must look in the right places and interpret one's findings in the right ways. This study locates the most significant data in the area of experimental ecumenical worship. It develops this data by means of a case study method designed to see the meaning of these acts in context. What are the implications of this approach?

2. THE SIGNIFICANCE OF EXPERIMENTS IN WORSHIP

Our concern is with new models of Christian gathering, indigenous to the new times in which we live. Why, then, concentrate on experimental forms of worship? The reason is that Communion and community are inseparable realities. It would be easy to study all kinds of Christian political involvements and theological innovations without being sure that the real issue was being faced. Where there is the celebration of Communion, and really only there, one can be sure that the question of the integral Christian reality in the world is, successfully or otherwise, being confronted.

The Swiss theologian J.-J. von Allmen makes the point precisely:

The Lord's Supper is a crucible which brings together all that makes the Gospel specific. . . . It is the one element of the Church's life which the world cannot reduce to that which is characteristic of itself.[5]

But this focus must not be misunderstood. This study proposes no withdrawal from political wrestling and no avoidance of theological difficulties. It may be just because these other issues are unresolved that worship today is so difficult and sometimes so irrelevant. On the other hand, it may be a flight from the problems, and the seemingly dead traditionalism, of familiar forms of worship that has sent many Christians into other kinds of activity in their search for what "church" can possibly mean for contemporary man. This whole bundle of issues must be held together. The real point may turn out to be that worship needs to be given a new social and intellectual location, outside what we have usually thought the "church" is, for it to come alive.

That worship, taken in and of itself, is a crisis area today is obvious. Members of the younger generation, including the new generation of clergy, are not sure they know how to pray, or even that they know what the idea, in a Christian context, should mean. Public worship palls, and innovations in this realm, however ingenious, may not reach the heart of the problem. What is more, the very idea of worship seems to get in the way of some of the most promising new adventures into Christian worldly responsibility. With the best intentions, a traditional act of worship may divide Christians from the very people they seek to serve. And ecclesiastical squabbles about sharing the Sacraments seem doomed to futility.

To those whose problems with worship are mainly personal, this study must not promise too much. It is natural for human beings to construe the question of prayer as one of communication with some power outside this world, or to think of it in terms of whether the petitions of men are "answered" by means of divine interventions in nature or history. Persons loaded with great personal burdens, wracked by inexplicable tragedy, want answers to such questions. They are understandably not interested in whether the symbol systems they use to ask the questions are products of vanished social realities or visions of the meaning of faith worked out in ages gone by. But these are precisely the questions that do have to be faced in the larger perspective. It is probable that answers to the personal questions cannot begin to be suggested today until these larger issues of social reality and symbol are tackled.

For the Biblical tradition the question about worship is not whether someone hears but to what end it is carried out. Worship is not just "talking to God." That is an incomplete impression left by the metaphors of the Biblical period. Worship is a matter of joining oneself to the whole Christian intention in history in terms of one's specific situation. The authentic Christian prayer is "Thy kingdom come." To pray such a prayer is to believe, ultimately, that man is not alone, that striving has meaning, that history has purpose. It is to believe in God. But it may not be to believe that God answers all manner of personal communications that the worshiper may care to transmit.

Much exciting experimentation in worship is going on. There seem to be situations in which the old traditions are coming alive and are being understood in new ways. These are the experiments that seem to offer not only possibilities in the renewal of worship as such but also suggestions concerning the renewal of the whole Christian reality, the authentic Christian presence, in the world. The purpose of this book is to probe such openings to see if they measure up to their promise.

3. THE USE OF THE CASE STUDY METHOD

It seems that the approach most likely to test these possibilities will be some form of the case study method. The style adopted here is simple narrative history accompanied by analysis and comment. Readers familiar with problems of method in the social sciences will be aware of what is involved. No questionnaires have been used, nor is there resort to statistical or quantitative method. It is hard to believe that even the most refined sociological techniques for gathering empirical evidence eliminate bias, and the straightforward method used here certainly does not. On the other hand, narrative history has the capability of reporting background, context, and nuance as no statistical method can. For purposes of this study, this seems all-important.

Some will feel, however, that the method chosen gives context an inordinate importance. This mode, as used in the field of ethics, is sometimes associated with the judgment that general rules cannot guide specific decisions. In "situational" or "contextual" ethics one tries to gather all materials for ethical judgment from the immediate circumstances, judging them in the light of some very general principle such as that of "what love requires." Is not the same thing being done here with the principle of "community"? Yes and no. The purpose is to see how the fundamental intention of Christian "communion" takes form in actual human settings. Thus the forms of gathering studied are those in which Christian words and acts play a primary role. But it must be remembered that the Christian norms themselves originated in particular contexts. Thus the origins of church attitudes and rules regarding Communion are *also* studied contextually. Sometimes norms developed in one context do not help us in another. In the end, an attempt is made to give a theological description of what goes on in the "indigenization" of Communion, whether in medieval Muscovy, in sixteenth-century Europe, or in contemporary America.

Publicity for experiments of the kind in this book could, of course, encourage others to try similar things, possibly without the right kinds of understanding and preparation. One commentator on the original research design called the project a "do-it-yourself manual for ecclesiastical disobedience." Such a peril exists. Many bishops know that experiments are going on in their dioceses, but are able to avoid disciplinary actions they would prefer not to take because the experimentation remains on a fairly small scale. An increase in such activity brought about by reading this book, or others like it, might have unfortunate results. Yet one cannot avoid the impression that history is passing the overly cautious prelates and church executives by. What was clandestine a few years ago is now out in the open. Nothing in this book, in fact, will come as a surprise to alert readers of the daily papers and the church press. The time has come for confronting the facts, and not for acts of discipline which, it is thought, will make the facts go away.

Nevertheless, a word is in order for those who may want to try ecumenical experiments for themselves. There is a difference between mere disobedience to church rule, the act of defiance and disrespect, and the act that challenges the church one loves to be faithful to its nature and mission. Every experiment in this book is of the latter kind, the only kind worth reporting and thinking about. The danger this report raises is not that more rules will be broken. It is that people may copy what has been done by others without going through the same practical experience or accepting the same spiritual responsibility. No model found in a book, and no atmosphere of permissiveness, can relieve a man of making his own decision on grounds of informed conscience. To argue precedent in matters of conscience is simply legalism all over again. Each new situation must be lived, and judged, afresh. Nothing in this or any other study can release a Christian from accountability for what he does to God, to himself, to his neighbor, and, if the case may be, to his bishop!

Whatever anyone may think of the experiments recorded here, they are significant to the church. There exists at present no really adequate criterion of faith or discipline for evaluating this material. The criterion must come, in some sense, from a sympathetic and discerning study of the experiments themselves. Thus the contextual approach is not only the preferred method, it is the only available one. Once it is understood what the experimenters are trying to do, once the common elements in these instances begin to be isolated, then theological judgments may begin to be made. Until then, and probably for much longer, we must keep open minds.

4. A Look Behind and Ahead

What has this study found? For those who would rather run than read, this much may be said: Research for this book began under the rubric of a rather forbidding Latin phrase which appears in Roman Catholic canon law. The phrase is *communicatio in sacris,* which, in its technical sense, means sharing by Christians of one tradition in the formal worship of another. This, at the time, seemed the best term to use for experiments going on outside church regulations. The object of the study was to examine closely existing experiments and existing rules, and to see what avenues there were in the situation for ecumenical progress.

Today, five years later, the situation is different. The difference can best be described by saying that we are less sure that new ecumenical developments can be accommodated within the gradual evolution of understanding that has marked formal theological conversations between the churches. Experimentation now seems more likely to break with institutionalized ecumenism than to be concerned about speeding it up. At the very least, experimentation is confronting ecumenical research with a set of problems that the category of *communicatio in sacris,* interpreted in traditional fashion, simply cannot cover. This Latin phrase must then take on a new set of meanings and associations, or cease to be used for the subject matter of the present study.

The shape of these new meanings is only beginning to appear, but some useful hints are at hand. A sacrum is a "holy thing." Increasingly the holy things of this life emerge in worldly rather than in ecclesiastical contexts, but they are no less holy for that. The holy appears where the events of history and the symbols of hope are linked together in a certain quality of common life that can only be responded to by celebration. Seldom, today, is the experience of the sacred a purely solitary, individual matter. The sacred is discerned in a certain kind of meeting that may be short-lived but whose nature is unmistakable.

Today there is no doubt that people, especially the young, long for "sacramental" experience of this kind. They have had enough of the very different approach to nature and history represented by the attempt to plan, manipulate, and control man and his environment. Acknowledging the benefits of technology, they refuse to construe the human world technologically. They see that man's formulas for mastering the course of history tend to ignore the deep bases of community, and to exploit the natural order. Long-range planning in such a revolutionary time may be a kind of conceit. There is, many now see, a different kind of expectation open to man that makes him sensitive to the quality of his common life and leads him to consecrate the natural world as his home. This kind of expectation need not lead to withdrawal from history: it leads to a kind of shared existence that can be lived in the midst of profound involvement. A group of Christians involved in the struggle for racial justice put it this way:

If in the racial revolution, as in other aspects of our contemporary social revolution, such weight is placed on life together in the midst of action, rather than upon rational articulation of long-range goals, the quality of this life together, the character of decisions made in the here and now, become incredibly important. What can sustain such a life? What can make such moments of decision rich and broad and deep? Only, we think, modes of celebration full of mystery and passion and telling symbolic acts. Without cultus, can individuals or groups bear the weight of life together, without long-range plans and the rational schemes that accompany them?[6]

Where such a level of life together is realized, even if it is only in a brief moment, people perhaps come as close as the modern world will allow to sharing in a sacrum. The whole creation is then seen in a certain light, in terms of a human meeting embodying a particular range of commitments. If and when this happens, it is something to be celebrated. Although it may not always be recognized as such, the Christian Communion service is designed as just such a celebration. The function of the liturgy is to illuminate the meaning of this sharing, to consecrate the bodily, material context in which it occurs, to situate man's striving where it can be nourished by hope. And if this can happen at all, it is possible to talk about *communicatio* in such *sacris*. For this term points to a wider, to a universal, sharing. The recognition that other communities, at other moments, have known the embodiment of the same possibility and have lived it in the same hope: this must go with the embodiment and the hope themselves.

In an age in which our communications networks are largely given over to the exchange of mere data, do we not need a medium for the universal sharing of sacra? Can the churches, as we know them, be such a medium? That is now the ecumenical question.

CHAPTER II

Christian Celebration
in the Midst of the World

THE EXPERIMENTS that have the most to teach us
tend to be those which have taken place outside the
environment or beyond the norms of the organized church.
It is not that other kinds of experiment are insignificant,
but the real question is whether communities of Christian
worship can be truly indigenous to the contemporary
world. The world must truly supply the context in which
Communion symbolism finds meaning. Experiments, therefore, that somehow carry traditional contexts with them
and that rest still on organic connections with the social
realities of a former time are not as valuable for our purposes as transplants that seem to have taken some kind of
root in the new environment of our day, surviving, if only
briefly, the rejection mechanisms that choke off such
attempts all too soon.

Do successful experiments of the latter kind really exist?
No known example fills the bill perfectly. The most that
can be said is that certain experiments illustrate certain of
the needed traits. None comes near to combining them all.
The decision about what materials to include is of course
bound to be partly arbitrary and therefore arguable. Instances that are included are not necessarily deemed more
important than others left out. Some occasions are related
mainly to provide historical perspective. Two broad categories, however, are not included at all, as much because

they have already been intensively studied as for any other reason.

Modern monastic or semimonastic communities such as Taizé, for example, are left aside. These represent an ancient form, and generally celebrate a liturgy deeply rooted in the past despite the highly contemporaneous nature of their worldly involvements. One has the impression that the strategy of such communities is to preserve a past social reality in all its fullness through the close-knit nature of a deliberately organized common life, and then to become involved in the modern social reality by sending its members out at other times to confront the world. The implications of this approach have been thoroughly analyzed elsewhere and need not be further studied here.

Similarly, it is impossible to give attention here to experiments that are essentially renewed versions of the parish community or local congregation. Many congregations such as the East Harlem Protestant Parish and the Church of the Savior have made great strides in learning how to interact with hostile environments and to orient the resources of the community to mission. But again, these are traditional forms operating in new ways. They have been elaborately described and evaluated in the literature of renewal and need not be investigated further now.

What remains is much harder to get hold of, and this is the object of the present study. Our interest is in community that forms, and becomes eucharistic, largely on the initiative of events and circumstances in the world: community that has not as yet been integrated into church programs and forms. This kind of community often has a short half-life. It may exist only for an hour. But it is extremely significant because in it we can see emerging forms of communion before they are ecclesiastically domesticated. Some of these short-lived forms may be those of the church of the future. They are those in which the really interesting and difficult problems arise.

1. THE PENTECOST EUCHARIST, PARIS, JUNE 2, 1968

The most striking examples of experimental break-through have taken place where Christians have tried to bear common witness in the midst of political crisis. The occasions have been many, for example, the little-publicized act of ecumenical Communion that took place in the street outside the Brown Memorial Church in Selma, Alabama, in April, 1965. The best-documented case, however, has been the common Eucharist involving Roman Catholics and Protestants, priests, ministers, and laymen, which took place in Paris at the time of the riots at Pentecost, 1968.

A great deal of information has been published about this, most of it in French. The most complete source, on which this account is based, is in the Protestant periodical *Christianisme Social,* Nos. 7–10, 1968.[7] On June 2, 1968, sixty-one persons, all of whom had, in varying degrees, been involved in support of the students and workers of Paris who were demonstrating in the streets for a liberalization of the French academic and economic systems, received Holy Communion at a simple celebration that took place in a private apartment on the rue de Vaugirard. From the Roman Catholic point of view, church discipline was violated in several ways: it is perhaps fairest to say that nothing in the legislation of that church then or now envisions either the liturgical form this celebration took, or the common Roman Catholic–Protestant leadership of the service, or the reception of the elements by members of both churches. The reception of both the bread and the wine of the Sacrament by the laity was unusual for Roman Catholics, but not unprecedented. From the Protestant side, while canon law was not broken, anti-Roman sensibilities were shocked.

Two thirds of the participants in this Eucharist were Roman Catholics. The service itself was based on a liturgy of St. Basil, an ancient text which both Protestants and Roman Catholics could share. An introduction was spoken, calling attention to the time it was both in the life of the church and in the life of the world. The Feast of Pentecost, symbol of the coming of the Spirit and the reunion of the People of God, was the churchly occasion. As for the world: Parisian students and workers were struggling for justice, while beyond, the struggle for freedom and independence went on in Algeria, Vietnam, and elsewhere, and the whole Third World was struggling for economic development. For several weeks, moreover, the participants had shared the "bread and wine of combat," including combat in the streets, as well as the "bread and wine of table fellowship." Under such circumstances, at the very moment when grace was at work, to have Holy Communion separately would be impossible. Yet those present who preferred not to receive the elements would be respected.

The service continued with Psalm 72, and Acts 2:1–39, followed by brief spontaneous comments on the Scripture and by spontaneous intercessions. Then followed the most liturgically innovative moment, a "eucharistic prayer," taking the place in the order of the Mass of the "prayer of consecration" and in Protestant services of the "words of institution" in their setting amid the circumstances of the Last Supper and Jesus' arrest. This eucharistic prayer was constructed in dramatic, responsive form. Three celebrants, Roman Catholic and Protestant, spoke portions of the prayer successively and then in unison, with unison responses by the whole people. The actual words of Jesus, "Take, eat; this is my body," and "Drink of it, all of you, for this is my blood," were spoken together by everyone present. In the *middle* of the eucharistic prayer as a liturgical response in itself, was a meditation on the meaning of the act by Paul Ricoeur. The kiss of peace, the Lord's Prayer, and then the bread and wine, received "in

both kinds" by sixty-one of those present, a final litany of
praise, and then the dismissal, "Let us go, proclaiming the
joy of Christ."

Paul Ricoeur's meditation, reconstructed from memory
by one of the participants, deserves special attention, not
only for the light it throws on the theological presupposi-
tions of the service but also because it was incorporated
into the liturgy, not made a kind of verbal-intellectual
adjunct to it. Ricoeur reflects that he knew that such a
moment, of leaping over the threshold of Holy Communion
together, would inevitably come. The way it had now come
was significant. The social revolution through which the
participants were living among the students and the
workers was actually *continuing* in the liturgy, for what
characterized this revolution was precisely a dialogue, a
sharing of the liberating, confronting, questioning, com-
missioning word that was gushing forth everywhere. This
was the real meaning of Pentecost, a festival of the shared
word. The attempt to build the Tower of Babel was an
attempt to create an artificial, cultural (i.e., verbal) unity,
and it had not come off. But Pentecost was the bursting out
of a profound unity, respectful of diversity, around a living
and creative word. Here were Roman Catholics and Protestants, with their whole cultural milieus and all their special
involvements, not united to be reduced to flat uniformity,
but one in the effort to discover the meaning of the word
in the light of shared worldly events. Other Christian traditions, the Orthodox, for example, were not actually represented but were not forgotten. It was vital to remember
that without the students and workers, we would not be
here. *They* were the decisive link between us. *They* made
the revolutionary act possible. Thus their "presence" was
to be compared with that of the bread and wine, products
of the work of unknown men. Those actually present were
now going to be nourished together, thanks to God, but
thanks to *them* too. Thus the Eucharist would send us

forth again with these brothers on the revolutionary road, in a dialogue that would bring out many levels of solidarity and communion in the encounter of both words and cultures, as together we sought to build a free world.

Ricoeur, on June 8, 1968, restated the central idea of this meditation in the French Protestant journal *Réforme*. In this form his words can be quoted in translation:

In the first place, this celebration was not the result of a desire to do violence [to church tradition]. It was "given" in the political situation, that is to say by a political impetus derived from the gospel itself, an impetus that verified the revolutionary import of the gospel for our time. Moreover, it was not only this particular event—the "May revolution"— but the world as such which gave us the opportunity to come together: the world, in the persons of these students and these workers alongside of whom we found ourselves in all kinds of ways during that extraordinary month. By becoming "third parties" between our separated Christian traditions, they threw together the bridge that our theologies and ecclesiologies have not yet built. So this Eucharist could crown a real community that existed before the celebration. In turn this community really began to exist, like a gesture thrown out ahead of us, before our theologies were in a position to delineate its theoretical shape. But don't things always happen this way? A community is born, it progresses by resort to risky acts. It makes the breakthrough, which the theologian then reflects upon and interprets.

In other words, the world enters significantly into the being of the church. It becomes in some manner the proper context of celebration, the locus of real presence, the significant setting of eucharistic sharing. The meaning of these claims will have to be carefully tested.

The public reaction to the June 2 Eucharist was surprisingly intense, judging from the volume of articles and letters that subsequently appeared not only in church publications both Roman Catholic and Protestant but also in

such secular daily newspapers as *Le Monde* and *Le Figaro.*
While the participants in the actual service had not sought
publicity for its own sake, they had immediately made the
move of sending identical letters to Msgr. François Marty,
Archbishop of Paris, and to M. Charles Westphal, President of the Protestant Federation of France. The wording
of the letter is significant at several points. The sixty-one
gathered for a purpose described functionally, rather than
institutionally: "to hear the Word together and to share
the eucharistic bread and wine." They had not planned
this gesture in advance; they had found themselves
"pushed" or "pressured" by the Spirit and by the circumstances. They had, in fact, "met" each other continually
among the students and workers in the streets. How could
they not celebrate the festival of "universal meeting,"
Pentecost, together? They did not know whether this was
an action they would have to repeat; certainly the struggle
for justice was continuing, and they intended to be part of
it. In solidarity with all those who were in the struggle,
they proclaimed "the death and resurrection of the Lord,
present and yet to come." The purpose of their letter was to
keep their common eucharist "just as far from loud publicity as from secrecy." The communication was signed by
all sixty-one communicants.

A brief declaration was also drafted by four other persons who had not received the bread and wine, but who
had been present and who wished to associate themselves
with the common prayer that took place. An unsigned and
somewhat poignant statement by another individual, by
declaration a Roman Catholic, accompanied this. Entitled
"Why I Did Not Take Communion," it confesses that the
Roman Catholic principle tying Holy Communion to the
visible church had been something he had just accepted,
not thought about very much and not held as a deep personal conviction. All the same, the Pentecost Eucharist
represented something unknown, something he did not

fully understand. He did not wish to be interpreted as taking exception to the significance found in the act by those who participated, but he could not, himself, communicate. "It is possible," this writer went on, "that if I had been more fully involved in the events during May which, for those weeks, united those who took part in this celebration, if, like them, I had experienced the profound unity of a faith confronted by the same [political] questions, if, in a word I had experienced the existence of an ecclesial community, sharing a common Christian conviction, growing up, as it were, from the ground, I would have joined the others in this risky action." But even this was not certain. A unity of faith felt in such circumstances, the need to make a common confession before the world: was it necessary to manifest these things in the form of a eucharistic meal? Moreover, was there not involved in this a somewhat premature Christianization of an essentially secular movement? Was this Eucharist not in effect the baptism of a revolution in which Christians might well see the action of God, but which was hardly interpreted this way by most of the revolutionaries? Yet there was a point to the celebration: there was a Pentecost of unity here. It just did not seem the right moment for a full participation.

Monsignor Marty, the Archbishop of Paris, quickly released a communiqué, which seems to have been a response to accounts of the Pentecost Eucharist in the public press, as it makes no reference to the letter sent him by the actual participants in the service. Acknowledging the extraordinary political events involved and the need for Christians to unite in common prayer, Msgr. Marty nonetheless indicated that he still could not condone a eucharistic form of worship in such circumstances so far as Roman Catholics were concerned. The Eucharist was the sacramental sign of a unity already realized, of an accomplished communion of life, thought, and feeling manifest in the confession of a common faith and in membership in the same church. Communion, moreover, was a liturgy of the universal church: it could not be based purely on the experience of a local community. This was why the Eucharist had to be celebrated in communion with the bishop, as representative of that universality. Obviously, then, Holy Communion was never a purely individual act. Only ordained priests had the power to consecrate the Eucharist, and this in virtue of their tie to the apostolic succession through the bishop. Moreover, unauthorized eucharistic acts ran the danger of creating new divisions, new "ecumenical communities" alongside the churches. For all these reasons, he could not "recognize" this gesture. There were other, more promising approaches to unity in which Catholics had the obligation to work.

Notably, the Archbishop did not, in this statement, take up the question of whether the Pentecost liturgy was or was not an actual celebration of Holy Communion. If anything, he assumes that it was. His point was that, as Archbishop of Paris, he could not "recognize" the act or "approve" of it so far as Catholics were concerned. He avoids the kind of language that might have been used in an earlier age: condemnation of the act as "false worship," and the like. This relatively irenic, but nonetheless ecclesiastically "correct" response won the approbation of the then President of the Vatican Secretariat for Christian Unity, Cardinal Bea, in a letter addressed to Msgr. Marty and subsequently published by the Secretariat. The Roman Catholic participants in the Pentecost liturgy were later received by the Archbishop, and so far as is known, no action was taken against them.

As for the official Protestant response, the Council of the French Protestant Federation passed a brief, unanimous resolution on June 9, 1968, noting that for Protestants the questions posed by a common Eucharist were not the same as those raised for the Roman Catholic Church. The whole range of concerns had been under study in dialogue with

Roman Catholics for some time. As for the particular motives and understandings connected with this particular celebration, the Council recommended that these be discussed by its member churches with the participants in the Pentecost Eucharist themselves.

On July 4, 1968, a joint Roman Catholic–Protestant committee met to consider the issues and to forward preliminary observations to the authorities of the churches concerned. This committee stressed the distinction between the admission of individuals of other churches to Communion and the actual celebration of Communion in common. The Pentecost event was one of the latter sort. Noting the great impatience, particularly among young people, with the barriers between the churches, this committee said it was not unthinkable that ways might be found to make common eucharistic acts possible. Above all, it was important that the churches should help people understand the profound significance of the Eucharist. The chasm between theologians and people should not be allowed to grow any wider.

Meanwhile, reaction from persons not immediately or officially concerned began to grow. On June 8, 1968, 268 priests and laymen signed a statement, published in *Le Figaro,* characterizing the Pentecost Eucharist as a "cry," a "summons," too long stifled, to the theologians and prelates. An event like this interpreted itself, and each individual could make his own estimate of its meaning, but a "cry" was something to be heard. The signatories knew that some people had been shocked by this "premature gesture," but, for them, the involvement in this Eucharist of those who had joined the revolutionaries in the streets had more weight than the querulous complaints of many church people. It was all very well to say "nothing can be done without the bishop," but through the whole history of ancient Israel, of the church, and of mankind, it was evident that nothing can be done without the people.

When the wind of revolution whips up the masses, the sign of Pentecost can be seen in an "insurrection of conscience."

This statement, it was soon made clear, was exactly what it said it was: the echoing of a "cry" by another "cry," not a theologically formulated argument in favor of intercommunion. A commentary by A. Aubry, one of the signatories, indicated that the purpose of the statement was to make clear to the authorities that they should take the Pentecost Eucharist seriously, that those who had participated were not just the ecclesiastical "Mafia." The theological weight of those concerned should make it difficult to close the case too soon. Above all, the public reaction should be carefully considered. Even though the Roman Catholic hierarchy had not condemned the action outright, it was clear that people in general had not grasped the point of the Archbishop's communiqué. The matter was therefore not finished. Even if, after close examination of the matter, it were necessary to conclude that the Pentecost Eucharist had been a mistake, that conclusion would not be as prophetic a word as the original liturgical gesture.

With the publication of these declarations, letters began to pour into the press. These defy summary, but several tendencies can be discerned. What strikes one immediately is the sheer effervescent joy of some, together with the absence of any spirit of disobedience or revolt for its own sake. Other letters dwell, sometimes at length, on the importance of prophetic action and risk-taking in the church. Still others, from priests and laity alike, indicate that the practice of intercommunion between Protestants and Catholics, at least to the extent of individuals receiving the Sacrament, is already fairly common in France and elsewhere. On the other hand, a considerable number of letters express feelings ranging from uneasiness to outright rejection of the Pentecost Eucharist. The fear most often articulated is that of a loss of the substance, the divine foundation, of the faith. Conditions in the world, these letters claim, do not justify eucharistic response. The reverse is true. The divine foundation of the faith and the episcopal authority that maintains and protects this faith must be kept in mind.

Equally, a number of theologians and ecclesiastical figures of note published commentaries within several weeks of the event. M. J. Le Guillou, Director of the Roman Catholic Institut Supérieur d'Études Oecumeniques, wrote in *La Croix* for June 19, 1968, that he found the Pentecost Eucharist not prophetic but ambiguous. The church, Père Le Guillou wrote, precedes and envelops us. It is not dependent on our human experience. And the Eucharist is absolutely inseparable from the church. The experience of a given group of Christians does not become normative for the church until it is judged to be so by the whole church. The Eucharist is not judged by experience; on the contrary, all human history is judged by the Eucharist. "Or, in other words, it is a question of deciding whether what is finally normative is the Church, built upon and by the Eucharist, or history as interpreted by groups or individuals." Whatever were the intentions of the participants, and whatever interpretations they placed upon the event itself, the eucharistic sign had its own meaning independent of all this: a meaning based on the intentions of Christ and the church. Père Le Guillou's article received the Pope's warm approval, conveyed in a letter of June 28, 1968, by Msgr. Benelli, of the Vatican Secretariat of State. Georges Casalis, one of the participants in the service and editor of the Protestant *Christianisme Social,* immediately took Père Le Guillou to task, however, for inaccuracies in representing both the event and the intention of those who were involved. It was not the case that the Protestants had invited the Catholics to be disloyal to their church. It was not the case that they conspired to manufacture a "prophetic act." The participants had been led by the Spirit to a common decision.

Moreover, it should not be thought that these communicants believed they were reinventing the church on the basis of their experience. They were convinced, rather, that Christ himself reinvented it every day, and that the problem was to be sensitive to this re-creation, this permanent revolution.

But not all cautionary comments came from the Roman Catholic side. Pastor Hébert Roux, writing in *Réforme* for June 22, 1968, clearly associates himself with those who feel that the political revolution of the Paris streets had positive elements, and with those who believe that within the church liberty comes before order. But he questions Paul Ricoeur's argument that the proper response to such convictions is the use of the Eucharist to "crown a true community" born of personal involvement in this revolution. What makes the community of Christian revolutionaries a truer community than some other? Is it because this community was born of political choice and political action? But did Jesus institute the Eucharist to sanction a political choice made by his disciples or did the gathering of the disciples *receive* its authenticity from Christ's action?

Furthermore, writes Roux, Ricoeur claims that such a deed has priority over theological interpretation. Theologians must subsequently make sense out of it. But does this not make a false antinomy between action and reflection, life and theology, as if theology did not take its departure from the same gospel as did prophetic action? What Christian action does not, consciously or otherwise, respond to some theological pressure? And if this is so, let no one say there was no implicit theology or ecclesiology behind this concelebrated Eucharist! Was there not, in fact, a danger of substituting new divisions for the lamentable confessional ones: divisions resting on other criteria which, if more contemporary, were not necessarily more evangelical?

All this was transformed, however, in a movement triggered by Prof. Johannes Hoekendijk, then of the University of Utrecht. In a defiant address, he poured scorn on "religion without decision," and on "the gospel as spiritual guide for pious souls in a little religious ghetto." "Are there no longer any revolutionaries among us?" he asked. "Are you ready, and do you really want, to work for the renewal of the Church in broader context of Kingdom and world?" The revolution Professor Hoekendijk demanded needed to begin in the ecumenical movement itself. "There will be no movement in the ecumenical movement until we are ready to venture forth from our traditions. . . . I appeal to you, for the love of God, be impatient and begin to practice this impossible thing called intercommunion."[8]

Professor Hoekendijk's address received an electric, almost ecstatic response from his hearers. On Friday, July 22, 1960, the act of intercommunion he had called for took place, outside the regular Conference program, in the Church of St. Francis. The Eucharist was an act of concelebration involving pastors from Reformed, Lutheran, Methodist, and united church bodies. Members and ministers of these and other Protestant groups received the Sacrament. Numerous Anglican and Orthodox priests and laymen were present and took part in the service, although it is not possible to say, for the record, how many of the latter actually received the bread and wine.

It is a sign of how rapidly events have moved that, as recently as 1960, an event such as this should have been greeted with both the acclamation in some circles and the dismay in others that followed. For leadership in the service was confined to ministers of relatively few churches, all of them "Protestant," and if Anglicans and Orthodox received the Sacrament as individuals, this was done on the basis of personal conscience, and not in such a way as to embarrass or commit their church authorities. The theological issues raised were essentially those of the

Reformed-Lutheran confrontation on the European continent, a debate going all the way back to the Marburg
Colloquy of 1529. This debate was, in effect, ended in
1957 at a Reformed-Lutheran meeting in Arnoldshain,
Germany, which produced the first agreed statement on the
meaning of Communion between these two confessional
groups. Despite the existence of this accord at the time of
the Lausanne celebration, a good deal of negative reaction,
from German Lutheran church authorities in particular,
followed the event. Official statements were made concerning the responsibilities of Lutheran students attending
ecumenical conferences. Yet the event has far over-
shadowed the official responses. At the time of this writing,
it seems a significant, but small, beginning of a movement
that has since grown greatly in scope and comprehensive-
ness.

b. *The University of Utrecht, 1960–1962*

Worship that takes place at ecumenical conferences
interacts with insights and experiments "at home." One of
the earlier significant developments of common eucharistic
worship in the university setting took place at Utrecht
University in the Netherlands, beginning in 1960 and
continuing for several years.[9] Significantly, this was Professor Hoekendijk's university. His presence and encouragement had much to do with the Utrecht events.

Initiative was taken in this case by the Universitaire
Kapeldiensten, a totally student-run Christian organization
in the university. Impatient with the languor of ecumenical
progress among the churches, this student movement began
to organize its own weekly services. The original purpose of
doing so was apparently double. The services were to be a
sign of the existence of a natural student community that
belonged together, and they were intended as a prod and a
challenge to the churches. In November, 1960, and with
the Lausanne ecumenical Eucharist in mind, the students

CHRISTIAN CELEBRATION IN THE WORLD   47

asked the authorities of several different church bodies in Utrecht to be responsible, in rotation, for the celebration of Communion in the student services. The request was, in effect, that these churches should celebrate the Sacrament in a fully "open" setting, permitting the student organization to be the effective ecclesial setting for the Eucharist.

Positive replies came from five churches: Reformed, Lutheran, Remonstrant (Congregationalist), Mennonite, and Moravian. The Old Catholics and two more conservative Reformed groups declined. Soon the churches that had replied affirmatively were asked to take a further step: not merely to celebrate alternately but to celebrate jointly—in short, to practice "concelebration." This, too, was agreed. Rapidly, therefore, and through the initiative of a student group, five otherwise separated churches found themselves practicing "intercelebration," a state of affairs considered a logical prelude to some form of organic union. In theory, what was now being practiced at the Communion table needed only to be ratified in the area of administration, and the churches would be one.

To the disappointment of the students, the churches did not take this administrative step, nor did their own Communion practice undergo any significant change. The most significant degree of unity among the churches that the students could urge into being was in the area of social service, where significant ecumenical moves were made. A similar disappointment attended the inability of this student group to make any headway in solving the problem of ecumenical worship with Roman Catholics. Only if the services were unofficial, nonchurchly meetings of individuals did it appear that Roman Catholics would be permitted to take part. This seemed to rule out the Eucharist, at least on the basis that had been set up. By 1962, therefore, this student movement faced an impasse. Ecumenism had to be conducted on two levels: one of social service in which all Christians could be involved and one of eucharistic worship in which only some Christians could be involved. The vision that a student organization, operating in the university rather than in the ecclesiastical setting, could actually bring about a solution to the churches' ecumenical difficulties seemed doomed to only partial realization.

Where was the basic error? In the period of self-examination that followed the flurry of activity from 1960 to 1962, the students noted that one of their assumptions had been that the answer to ecumenical puzzles would lie in the discovery of the right ecumenical institutional form, and that they had had the temerity to think they could provide it. Perhaps, the journal articles of this period suggested, the church comes into existence only at the point of contact between the gospel and the world. If so, the church comes to be in different ways at different times. Institutional unity in itself is not in this case an object to be sought. It is important to concern oneself with other churches only where one meets with them at the worldly intersections. The primary object is service and witness, not trying to be an institution for the promotion of church unity. After all, what is the real ecumenical problem? Is it the fact that different Christian groups exist, or is it that they fence themselves off from one another in an absolutist way? The discussion in Utrecht thus moved in the direction of an action and service-oriented ecumenical pluralism, which, in turn, led to the insight that *all* ecclesiastical forms and fellowships needed to justify their existence operationally. If they were involved in the mission of the church, they *were* the church. Emphasis shifted from the role of this student group in uniting the existing "denominations" to a consciousness within the group that it, itself, was either an ecclesial reality or nothing. The purpose of keeping in touch with the traditional churches was no longer that of gaining ecclesiastical legitimacy through their sponsorship. It was now that of making clear the ecclesiological implications, valid for all churches, of this student group's own existence as a serving, worshiping community, a community existing both inside and outside the traditional church organizations.

Ecumenical discussion in the Netherlands has since shifted away from this pioneering experiment, largely because of the opening of new possibilities of relationship with Roman Catholics, and these not only in the universities but at the parish level. This is clearly a matter of a different kind, to be discussed elsewhere. The significance of the Utrecht experiment, and of similar experiences at other Dutch universities, is that it marks a further step along a particular ecumenical way, carried still farther in student contexts in more recent years.

c. *Athens, Ohio, December 31, 1963*

The Nineteenth Ecumenical Student Conference, sponsored by the National Student Christian Federation and the World Student Christian Federation, which met at Ohio University in Athens, Ohio, over New Year's weekend, 1963–1964, was in many ways a North American parallel to the European Youth Assembly in Lausanne three years before. The attention of the meeting was sharply focused on social and political problems: in this case, above all, the question of racial justice, for this meeting took place as the participation of the churches in the American civil rights movement was reaching a high point. The March on Washington on August 28, 1963, had taken place four months previously. Martin Luther King's "I have a dream" speech, uttered on that occasion, was still ringing in the conference's ears. Three months later the demonstrations in St. Augustine, Florida, under Dr. King's leadership, were to begin. The ecumenical Eucharist at Athens took place in a worldly context in at least this sense: that the thoughts of the participants, fed by the many words spoken both within and outside the actual service, were being turned decisively outward toward the question of practical approaches to social justice.

The Athens Eucharist differed from that of Lausanne, however, in not being conceived and executed on the spot. On the contrary, the leadership of this meeting, gathered around Bishop Daniel Corrigan, of the Home Department of the Protestant Episcopal Church, began to lay plans for an ecumenical celebration of the Eucharist a year before the conference met.[10] Bishop Corrigan was determined to arrange a celebration that would encourage maximum participation by those actually attending the conference. This, he felt, would not be accomplished by involving large numbers of ecclesiastical executives, who would not be present, in dialogue concerning exceptions to church rules, but by conceiving of the most authentic possible form of the Eucharist within the conference setting and in relation to the conference's concerns. Thus, although church executives such as the Protestant Episcopal Bishop of Southern Ohio knew of the plans, and tended personally to encourage them, the matter was never brought before such officials for formal decision, which might have had to be negative. (Ministers of the Protestant Episcopal Church, for example, are officially required to use the Communion liturgy of the Book of Common Prayer, which was not the form employed on this occasion.) There was thus a sense in which the effective church for this celebration was not identifiable with any denomination, and a sense in which this ecumenical fact was openly celebrated by those concerned.

The liturgy for the occasion was chosen with these requirements in mind. The involvement of Dr. H. Boone Porter, a liturgical scholar at the General Theological Seminary in New York, opened a door to the adaptation of a Communion liturgy older than any of the divisions that now separate Christians: the Liturgy of Hippolytus, which represents the late second century. The service actually used, of course, was a reconstruction, by Dr. Porter and others, partly based on known Hippolytan texts, partly based on descriptions of ancient Christian worship given by Justin Martyr and on the directions given in the Apostolic Constitutions, and partly adapted with modern materials. The major advantage of the Hippolytan liturgy for this occasion, apart from its age, was that it is designed to be performed by a group of celebrants, and not by an individual. Thus without any artificial distortion of the structure of the rite, it was possible to have a large number of ministers of different denominations take part in the consecration of the elements.

The idea of "concelebration" here, of course, was not originally intended as a device for circumventing ecclesiastical regulations in a divided church. Rather the point was that in the Eucharist different members of the assembly do different things, just as different members of the body of Christ have different functions in mission. The celebration is inherently a corporate act. Whether persons other than clergy are to be considered as concelebrating in *their* roles in the service is left unclear by modern commentators. But the basic point is that the corporate nature of the service precludes any notion of the minister as performer on the platform, and the congregation as audience in their seats. Thus the ancient idea of concelebration was now put to new use. Was there any reason why the participants in this corporate celebration could not be ministers of different denominations? And did this not offer a way of joining these different ministrations, however they might be understood, into a single eucharistic action?

This, at any rate, was the Athens insight. The actual celebration of the Eucharist involved twenty-four ministers, of a wide variety of denominations, with Bishop Corrigan acting as president of the assembly. More ministers assisted with the distribution of the elements from small tables stationed throughout the gathering of three thousand. One representative of each of the one hundred study groups at the conference participated in the offertory, with the specific implication that the intellectual work of the meeting was being offered up in the Sacrament. The central issue, however, was confronted in the handling of the eucharistic prayer, or prayer of consecration. It is here that the most significant differences of view among the churches are concentrated. At Athens the Hippolytan prayer was recited by Bishop Corrigan, while the other twenty-four presbyters around the large table were understood to be joining in prayer silently, and thus as officiating at the celebration along with Bishop Corrigan in the fullest sense. Still, it was also understood that these ministers could pray what they wanted to pray. In other words, those who could identify themselves wholly with the prayer of Hippolytus would do so, while those who felt that the traditions of their own churches required them to be reciting some other words, or additional words, or fewer words, would be understood to be doing that. All the ministers, however, were understood to be responsible together for consecrating all the elements. It was not that some of the bread and wine was set aside for Lutherans, and some for Episcopalians, and so on. The latter possibility had been considered in the planning sessions, and was rejected both as too cumbersome and as theologically unnecessary.

The best guesses of persons who were present indicate that at least two thousand people received the Sacrament. These seemingly included at least some Roman Catholic and Orthodox participants, although ministers of these two communions were not included among the twenty-four consecrators. For nearly every church and communion represented, however, there was at least *some* theological difficulty in this celebration. Lutherans had difficulty with the offertory, Methodists with the use of wine, Episcopalians with the use of an unapproved liturgy, and so on.

The greater difficulties of Roman Catholics and Orthodox were of a somewhat different kind, centering above all in the fact that this service was not authorized by their church authorities, and did not take place within the true eucharistic fellowship as their communions defined it. What overcame the difficulties for those who received the Sacrament was not, for the most part, the ingenuity of the celebration itself. The construction and enactment of the liturgy merely made the difficulties less obtrusive. What overcame the difficulties was the context in which the service took place: a context of study and fellowship in which the church was being constantly turned outward toward the world both in the subject matter of the meeting and in the ethical intentions formed there. In other words, the same liturgical form celebrated in exactly the same outward way would not, in another context, have been the same eucharistic *act*. The context was all-important.

In the considerable flurry of public interest that followed the Athens Eucharist this fact tended to be overlooked. Requests poured in for copies of the Hippolytan liturgy, as if this service had some magical ecumenical property. It was necessary for Professor Porter to mimeograph a form letter stressing the contextual element, but even this was not enough to prevent misunderstanding. Surprisingly, seven months after the event, *The New York Times* revived public interest in the Hippolytan liturgy as a kind of ecumenical stratagem. On August 1, 1964, George Dugan wrote in the *Times* as follows:

A simple religious rite more than 1700 years old may provide the answer to how Christians, divided for centuries, may once again receive together the central sacrament of their faith: holy communion.

Should Roman Catholic, Protestant, and Eastern Orthodox theologians accept a modern adaptation of the ancient rite—and there is every reason to believe that many of them will—

it could constitute an important breakthrough in the search for Christian unity.

The fact of the matter was, however, that what made the celebration of the Eucharist at Athens a breakthrough was the long preparation of the rite in the context of world-oriented conference planning by a group of Christians who trusted each other; and then the sensitivity of this group, led by Bishop Corrigan, in explaining the proposed Eucharist in such a way that it became an integral part of the meeting. Anyone willing to live through and live out such a contextual preparation could very well make the same ecumenical "breakthrough." Some liturgy other than the Hippolytan then might serve as well.

d. *Basel, Switzerland, September 8, 1967*

In September, 1967, a conference on "Christian Presence in Higher Education" took place in Basel, Switzerland, under the joint auspices of the Conference of European Churches and the World Student Christian Federation.[11] The double sponsorship was significant in itself, for the meeting was to some extent an encounter between students, student movement leaders, and representatives of the churches. Again, the meeting was world-oriented: the topic had to do with the university as an arena of human interaction and with the role of Christians in such a context. The act of eucharistic worship at the close of the meeting was designed to catch up, in liturgical form, what the gathering had been about and to relate all this to the fundamental bases of Christian obedience.

Compared with the Athens assembly, this consultation was much smaller, and consisted of a somewhat older and more theologically experienced group of people. On the other hand, a greater variety of languages and national backgrounds was represented, a fact that threatened difficulties in mutual understanding of another kind. The liturgy used and the procedures followed were, on the whole, much less consciously constructed to minimize official ecclesiastical discomfort. But just as much care was taken to plan in advance, and, above all, to explain to potential participants just what the service meant in its particular conference setting.

The planners produced a fascinating essay on these subjects which was distributed to the meeting in advance. The circulation of this paper was "seen as an integral part of the plan" for the ecumenical Eucharist. The planning committee was "anxious that no one in any way involved shall be taken unawares, but that each member of the consultation shall be able to give careful thought to the plans and their implications: to do this, moreover, within the church and thus to consult the appropriate authorities of his own confession, if he feels it necessary to do so, to seek their advice and to keep them informed." The paper acknowledged the heavy pastoral responsibilities assumed by the planners of the conference, and went on to say: "We realize that many members of the conference are going to find it very difficult to make up their minds whether to partake of the bread and wine or not. But the burden of this decision, in the nature of the case, cannot be assumed by the conference. It must rest on the delegate and on those who interpret the discipline of his church to him."

The paper then went on to summarize the history of the question, pointing out that meetings of the WSCF had been among the earliest contexts in which the issue was raised. Communion used to be served to everyone. It was only when the churches, as such, became participants in the ecumenical movement and a wider range of confessions was represented that the difficulties became apparent. Reflection and pioneering practice within the WSCF had made a major contribution to thinking within the World Council of Churches, particularly in the Lund (1952) and Montreal (1963) decisions on Holy Communion at ecumenical conferences. Now the WSCF was moving ahead again with a policy developed by its General Committee at Córdoba, Argentina, in 1964. This was expressed, in part, as follows:

We are clear that there can be no full and final solution to the question until our churches are fully and finally united in faith. We are clear, too, that no advance can be made by any sort of unilateral decision on the part of the WSCF, and we shall therefore not try to lay down exactly what shall and shall not happen at WSCF conferences. . . .

Therefore we envisage a fully and deliberately pastoral approach, in which the criteria for decision in any situation will be based on a pastoral assessment by the planners of the conference and by the appropriate authorities in the churches of the readiness and maturity in Christ of the particular people and situation involved, and in which the practice adopted will never be more than partial and temporary. Further, it must be so arranged as to contribute to the building up of the total community rather than to its further division. What is primary for us is that each group, united in their Christian obedience, be able to worship openly and with integrity; we are not asking, indeed we renounce, that the sacrament be used as an educational device. Integrity here cannot be exactly defined, but it has to do with the service, *and* with the context of the service.

Now, at Basel in 1967, the planners continued, one could sense "a marked shift in opinion." "Whereas in the past planners have had to recognize that many would be unable for reasons of conscience to participate fully in a common service, now they must take note of the many for whom it is a question of conscience not to take part in anything less." A major new feature of the Basel meeting was the substantial number of Roman Catholic participants, perhaps one in six of the total present. Did this make a basic difference? The committee concluded that it did not. Like anyone else, the Roman Catholics would have to make their own decisions in conscience, and in this they would not face any problem substantially different from those with which others, particularly Anglicans and Orthodox, had long been familiar.

As for the authorization of the service, all that could be said was that the text of the liturgy made it abundantly clear that the intention was to obey Christ's command, that the celebrant of the service had been asked to officiate by the conference planning committee and was seeking the explicit authorization of his church, the Church of Sweden, to do so, and that a body representing the Christian community in the place of the meeting, the Evangelical-Reformed Church of Basel had given its general assent to the plan and had notified the other churches in the city about it.

Discussion of these considerations and their relevance was not suppressed but encouraged in the course of the meeting. It has to be said, however, that the consultation was so immersed in issues not lending themselves to discussion in theological, let alone eucharistic, language, that the fact of a common celebration of the Sacrament was more assumed by the delegates as a natural thing to do than avidly discussed. Permission came from the Bishop of Lund, on condition that the Apostles' Creed or the Nicene Creed be used in place of the contemporary one borrowed from a Roman Catholic community in Leiden, the Netherlands, which the planners had wanted to employ. There is no doubt that many Roman Catholics received the Sacrament, including more than one priest. The Roman Catholic university chaplain from Leiden, Jan van Well, who had been a member of the planning group, shared in the administration of the elements alongside a Baptist woman pastor.

In general, it would seem that the service was received with enthusiasm, but without much subsequent theological comment. The single point one notices is that again the Orthodox were unable to be involved either in the planning or in the celebration itself. What does this fact mean from the ecumenical standpoint? Should churchmen of a liturgical tradition, such as the Orthodox, prefer that the conference celebrate a liturgy even if they cannot join it? Or would a lesser act of worship, in which all could have joined, have been preferable?

e. *The Shift Toward Local Initiative*

It is noticeable that somewhere about 1965 or 1966 the scene of liturgical experiment in student groups began to shift, and with it the nature of the experiments. Doubt began to be expressed about the very propriety of large student assemblies, and local campus groups began to intensify their efforts to carry on eucharistic worship on an ecumenical basis. In this shift of emphasis, the earlier experiments at Utrecht obviously pioneered. But the Utrecht type of experiment, with its early emphasis on leading the churches to take formal ecumenical action, did not become widespread because the conclusions subsequently reached in Utrecht itself soon were echoed in many quarters: namely, that the real issue is not that of finding clever liturgical devices to circumvent or minimize church rules; it is that of creating a genuinely eucharistic community in the first place.

Any adequate charting of the plethora of local eucharistic experiment in student circles is out of the question. It is so because complete documentation does not exist, because experiments have often been *ad hoc,* short-lived, and unrecorded. Nevertheless, enough is known to indicate the direction in which events are moving. The direction is toward greater and greater freedom of interaction across church lines. Seemingly, it can be said that any imaginable form of eucharistic sharing involving Protestants and Roman Catholics has now been tried somewhere. Orthodox priests and students have been involved in this sharing, but less actively.

The range of possibilities runs from common participation in noneucharistic services to Protestant and Roman Catholic concelebration of a formal eucharistic rite. Commonly, the experiments run somewhere in between. It has become common for Protestant students both to attend Mass, and to receive the Sacrament on occasion. Roman Catholics, less frequently, have received the Sacrament at Protestant services, particularly Episcopal celebrations according to the Book of Common Prayer. Protestant ministers have been asked to read the lessons at Mass, and on occasion have been invited to take part in the Offertory in which the Host, or Communion wafers, are brought forward to the altar. Conversely it has occurred that Roman Catholic priests, assisting in the leadership of a eucharistic service other than the Mass, have not only participated in a unison saying of the prayer of consecration, but have also assisted in the distribution of the elements, both bread and wine, to the congregation.

Increasingly the feeling is that complex advance planning and the securing of official permissions (in contrast to the building of actual local communities of confidence and understanding) is of little importance. The community to be honored is the immediate one, the local one. This is done without any intention of disowning allegiance to one's own particular communion. It is simply increasingly felt and said that eucharistic community comes into being in a manner congruent with actual human community, and is in some ways a celebration of it.

One naturally moves from this to the possibility that there will be persons present in the natural student community, persons who have shared the ethical intentionality responsible for bringing the community into being, who wonder if they can take part in eucharistic celebrations even if they are not professing, baptized Christians. Such

situations force upon Christian ministers the choice of celebrating the Sacrament in such a way as to divide the
natural community, or of abstaining from the Eucharist in
such contexts altogether. Responses seem almost equally
divided between these two possibilities. There is no doubt,
however, that under some circumstances the Eucharist is
being used in a missionary mode, in which all who happen
to be present are made welcome if they wish to participate.

One such celebration took place in the chapel of a
college in New England at the time of the death of Dr.
Martin Luther King, Jr. A highly diverse company of students and faculty, Christians, Jews, agnostics, and atheists,
had committed themselves to a three-day fast in honor of
Dr. King and as a public demand for action on a series of
issues concerned with racial justice. The chaplain of the
college felt moved to invite this group to end their fast
with a common meal of bread and wine in the sanctuary.
To his combined surprise and joy, a large number of the
fasters, representing every persuasion, came. Readings
from Scripture and from other sources were provided by
members of the group: readings that included Isaiah's Song
of the Servant and Matthew's account of the Last Supper.
Fresh French bread and a good red wine, in quantity, were
passed from hand to hand. One participant, so hungry he
could hardly contain himself, exclaimed that he could
smell the bread and wine coming five rows away! "I think,"
he said, "that I understand something."

This, of course, was an occasion of extraordinary emotional tension. For the campus in question the event was
unique. More common have been much smaller celebrations with bread and wine, contemporary music, dance,
free prayer, and meditation, which make no formal attempt
to be eucharistic in any recognized churchly way, but
which are nevertheless unmistakably the Christian feast.
For these no ordained clergyman is thought needed, and
complex theological argument is simply out of place.

Equally significant, however, is the tendency of some Christians in university settings to feel that their involvement in the life of the academic community has begun to make the Eucharist irrelevant in *any* form. Thus the recent revolutionary events on American university campuses have produced fewer liturgical experiments than might have been expected. The question of whether there *can* be an authentic eucharistic community, and, if so, where such a community can be found or how it could be gathered, now becomes the issue. Some things said at the Basel consultation of the World Student Christian Federation and the Conference of European Churches now seem to be borne out.

There are many who in the end find experimental forms hardly more authentic than the original. . . . It is quite conceivable that in the university Christian communities of the future . . . there will be no explicit acts of worship but at best what has been called "a great silence," within which Christians can get on with unassuming acts of neighborly service.

And again:

It is entirely appropriate that the more "radical" of Christians in the academic world, those that are really searching for the roots, should feel that their reasonable worship is in active obedience, in doing their academic work well or in pursuing university reform; that it is in sharing in the making of decisions about the future that they show forth the worth of Jesus.

3. SMALLER ECUMENICAL MEETINGS

Breakthroughs in common worship have not generally taken place in the context of large ecumenical conferences, nor have they often happened at gatherings where the subject under discussion was "worship" or "intercommunion" as such. The rule that actual progress has been made where the major preoccupation has been worldly or practical is not broken even in the case of meetings consisting mainly of church executives, clergy, or members of religious orders.

Thus the great Faith and Order meetings that formulated the existing recommendations for Holy Communion at ecumenical gatherings (Lund, 1952, and Montreal, 1963) and the World Council of Churches Assemblies that endorsed these recommendations and carried them out (Evanston, 1954; New Delhi, 1961; Uppsala, 1968) have not been scenes of astounding advance. Nor have consultations convened within the Faith and Order movement to talk about this very subject. In the case of the large meetings, the public visibility of the events and the fact that participants have been official representatives of their churches have blocked the bold steps that some have wanted to take. In the case of the "intercommunion" consultations there has undoubtedly been a fear that the act of celebrating an ecumenical Eucharist might either force, or romanticize, a discussion that requires realism about the actual situation among the churches.

As far as meetings of these types have been concerned, the "Lund" and "Montreal" rules have been followed. Two celebrations are suggested within the conference program but not under conference sponsorship: one celebration authorized and carried out by a church able to issue an open invitation to all participants and one by a church unable to issue such an invitation, with all conference participants urged to *attend* both Eucharists but to receive according to conscience and the rules of their own communions and confessions. Other eucharistic celebrations, apart from the conference schedule, are also possible, under these recommendations, on request. Such a policy accurately reflects the *official* situation in interchurch relationships at the present time. It limits progress beyond this situation to the level of personal decisions that individuals may make. Progress of this limited kind there certainly has been at the major meetings, but it hardly figures in the present discussion.

A different situation, however, is beginning to obtain at ecumenical meetings of smaller size dealing with other topics. A few examples will illustrate this tendency.

a. *Arlington Heights, Massachusetts, August, 1965*

An annual series of meetings of members of Episcopalian and Roman Catholic religious orders has taken place at the Convent of St. Anne, in Arlington Heights, Massachusetts, beginning in August, 1965. From the restricted scope of the original plans for these meetings to the eucharistic sharing that subsequently took place, a dramatic development, typical of the rapid movement of the question today, is plainly evident.

Plans for the 1965 meeting[12] were that this conference of some eighty men and women religious, equal numbers of Roman Catholics and Episcopalians, would celebrate the Sacrament on alternate days according to the Roman Catholic and Episcopal orders. All participants would attend each other's Eucharists, and would be united in the daily chanting of the Benedictine *Shorter Breviary*. It was not foreseen that members of the two churches would receive the Sacrament together. Fellowship in the Sacrament was to be symbolized, instead, by the sign of *pain bénit*: trays of rolls were carried to the sanctuary step in the Offertory Procession by Episcopalians at the Mass, and by Roman Catholics at the Episcopal celebration, and then consumed at the following *agapē* meal. Likewise, at each celebration the kiss of peace was given throughout the community.

Life together in the conference, however, seemed to generate an inner pressure for something more. As one participant afterward wrote:

Three times, while we Anglicans were receiving Holy Communion and our Roman Catholic brothers were unable to do so, the latter sang (through tears), "One Church, united in Communion blest," all of us realizing the ghastly falseness of the words. After that we would have preferred a penitential fast to an agape breakfast.

A decision was therefore reached, in the course of the meeting, to overcome this separation at least for the eucharistic celebration on the Feast of the Transfiguration, which was to be the keynote and climax of the week. At the initiative of Father Paul Wessinger, an Episcopal priest, it was proposed that the Episcopalians might at least receive the elements from their reserved Sacrament after the Roman Catholic Mass. Father Edward Hennessy, the Roman Catholic who was to celebrate the Mass, was willing to go one step farther. The Episcopalians might receive their reserved Sacrament not after but at the same time as the Roman Catholics were communicating, that is to say, within the Roman Catholic liturgy. And not only this, the Roman Catholics, on this occasion, would receive both bread and wine, as Episcopalians did normally. At the Mass, Episcopalians and Catholics formed one line, separating only at the altar to go right or left to receive from priests of their own communion.

Significantly, subsequent joint Anglican–Roman Catholic meetings in this series have not repeated the same device of using the reserved Sacrament as a way of receiving Communion together without formally transgressing church rules. While there has apparently been no act of concelebration, some of the participants now feel free simply to receive Communion at the altar in the celebrations of the church other than their own.

This is the progression which, on the basis of experience elsewhere, one would expect. Any act that in any way breaches the line between the churches tends to lead to other such acts, to a greater boldness, and to a greater freedom. Ingenious devices for circumventing rules, however sincerely and worshipfully meant in their original contexts, now give way to a frank sharing of Communion by those who feel ready to do so. In a sense, of course, this raises fewer problems than acts that approach common celebration, for individual reception of the Sacrament can be accommodated by stretching present rules having to do with cases of special need. One can anticipate, however, that development in this direction will move still farther to the point of one celebration for all: if not in this particular series of meetings, certainly in one like it before long.

b. *Medellin, Colombia, September 5, 1968*

In September, 1968, at the Second Assembly of the Roman Catholic bishops of Latin America, five Protestant observers formally requested and formally were granted permission to receive the Sacrament at Mass the day before the end of the conference.[13] While non-Roman Catholics have received the Sacrament at Mass before, and, indeed, this is no longer unusual, given the requisite circumstances and where individual persons are concerned, it would appear that the event at Medellin was the first case of an explicit, written authorization by the Roman Catholic hierarchy in response to a no less explicit written request.

Eleven observers had been present throughout the meeting and had participated fully in its work: attending section meetings and acts of worship alike. Reduced in numbers to five by the final days of the conference, the observers met to draft a statement, which had been invited by the bishops, for presentation at the closing plenary session. One of the paragraphs of this statement alluded to the observers' regret that all present had not been able to share the Eucharist together. The five rather suddenly found themselves unanimous in sensing that the moment had come for more than regrets: a sign, an appeal, was in order. They had shared a piece of life with the Catholic

bishops; why not Holy Communion as well? Accordingly
the group drafted a letter to the bishops, alluding to their
presence at Mass each day of the conference. Could they
not actually receive the Sacrament on one occasion? The
letter included quotations from the recent *Directory* published by the Vatican Secretariat for Christian Unity. The
five indicated that their case could well be considered
under the heading of "urgent necessity," for what could be
more urgent than love? The *Directory* also mentioned
"other cases of urgency" and left it to the diocesan bishop,
or episcopal conference, to decide what such cases might
include. As for the five, they could assure the bishops that
they stood in substantial unity of faith with regard to the
church's understanding of the Sacrament. They could all
affirm their faith in the words of the 1968 *Consensus* of
the views of representative theologians prepared by the
Faith and Order Department of the World Council of
Churches.

Significantly, the stance taken by these five Protestants
stressed their solidarity with their own churches. Their
initiative, they said, was not to be taken to mean that as
individuals they were doing something that should be
interpreted as separatism. On the contrary, they could each
affirm that they were acting as faithful members of their
own confessions. Such an insistence was necessary not only
to avoid any appearance of disloyalty but also to lend
heightened ecclesial significance to whatever answer the
Roman Catholic bishops might give.

The reply was not long in coming: in the affirmative.
The bishops made but one request, that the five not come
to the altar as a group, but that they come forward naturally with all the others receiving the Sacrament that
evening.

The Medellin initiative proved to be controversial, and
it is still under discussion. Was this a proper interpretation
by the bishops of the intention of Vatican II and of the

Directory (see the discussion of these documents in Chapter III)? Did the action of the five actually fall within the bounds of loyalty to their own churches? At least one highly placed Roman Catholic observer has since expressed his doubt. On September 18, 1968, Paul VI listed "acts of intercommunion contrary to good ecumenical principles" in a list of ills in the modern world, such as political violence, pornographic films, and opposition to his encyclical on birth control.

4. THE UNDERGROUND CHURCH

Malcolm Boyd has defined the underground church as "a contemporary Christian revolutionary movement . . . bypassing official Church structures and leadership, and concerned with Christian unity and radical involvement in the world."[14] In general, members of underground Christian communities are people who have fled, permanently or temporarily, the traditional institution to try to create new forms of gathering in a secular context. The word "underground" is not necessarily descriptive. For the most part there is nothing secret about the movement. Other observers have proposed that these communities be called "free" churches (Rosemary Reuther) or "group" churches (the sociologist Rocco Caporale, S.J.). These bodies are not parishes that have discovered a new mission to be performed within existing, or somewhat modified, structures. They are groups that specifically dissociate themselves from the organized church. As Caporale puts it, they are "covenanting ecclesial units, neither territorially nor hierarchically located, which maintain functional identity boundaries, and generate more or less enduring autonomous systems of symbolism, control, and rewards."[15] The majority of members of underground congregations are Roman Catholic, but there are numerous Protestants involved as well.

As contexts for the celebration of Holy Communion, these bodies represent fascinating case studies. Like the other experiments here examined, they represent deliberate attempts to resituate the eucharistic tradition in the contemporary worldly environment. The kind of eucharistic context they afford is one that plays down formal channels of organization and authority, that plays up interpersonal communications and the search for a profound quality of community life.

The underground, of course, is not limited to worshiping groups. There is also, as William Hamilton has pointed out, a *theological* underground and an underground of *ethical witness,* members of which may or may not participate in worship. These groups overlap with the *liturgical* underground, offering it both intellectual and moral support. The common conviction of all forms of the underground is "that in the name of Christian renewal and authenticity one must go one's own way often without support from the institutional church and, as the case may be, against it. Initiative does not rest in the institutional church and its authorities and does not respect traditional structures."[16]

The *liturgical* underground receives most attention here for reasons already set forth in Chapter I. In liturgy the intention to be in some sense the church becomes most socially visible. For a variety of reasons, however, it is difficult to select one or two from the thousands of such communities that now exist for case study. Instead, let us take a composite case, a kind of ideal type, and describe it in the words of one who has observed many such instances at first hand:

The setting may be very simple: a family has invited some friends, relatives, and neighbors. They sit around the dining room table. The priest, a friend of the family, dressed in shirt and tie, presides over this meeting. He reads a passage or two from the Bible and opens a discussion. The liturgy can be adapted to respond to a personal situation—for example, the first communion of a child—or to a national calamity such as the death of Dr. Martin Luther King, Jr. Prayers are said, each contributing his own particular concern. There may be some singing.

The text of the canon for the mass is one of the twenty-odd mimeographed versions that are circulating now among priests and lay people. Each participant receives both bread and wine, the cup being passed around to everyone; the bread and wine were bought in a grocery store in the neighborhood. The children have a sip of wine before so they know its taste. The atmosphere is relaxed, yet solemn. These are people who know each other; they are friends, but what they do now is special, not simply a meal or a cocktail party. They *celebrate* a deeper concern for each other. The search is for community in Christ.[17]

Within this general format there is great variety. The liturgy used may be that of the Mass in every detail, or it may come close to being extemporaneous worship. The theological tone may range from mystical celebration of the presence of Christ to a distinct emphasis on social and ethical commitment. The group may be entirely Roman Catholic, but it may very well not be. Some underground groups are consciously "ecumenical" in the sense of being both Protestant and Roman Catholic. Leadership may be that of the ordained priest, the ex-priest, the Protestant minister, the ex-minister or simply "lay" as far as churchly status is concerned.

One of the real possibilities in the underground movement is concelebration, in the sense earlier discussed. The basic idea is intrinsic to the house church form: the whole assembly carries out the sacramental act. The people do not merely receive the Sacrament, they celebrate it. Thus the composition of the community already determines the ecumenical character of the Communion. For a Protestant and a Roman Catholic, lay or ordained, to share the liturgical leadership of such a group is an obvious step. What is

awkward and unnatural in the traditional church setting
becomes a matter of course in the underground format.
No protest need be involved. It is simply the natural thing
to do.

So far, the underground communities show little or no
desire to be separate from the church at large. There is, on
the contrary, a very high degree of loyalty to the wider
Christian community: a determination to see the movement as something happening within the church, not
outside it. Moreover there persists the hope that such a
movement within the church may be a significant agency
of reform. On the Roman Catholic side, there is a record of
attempts by underground communities to establish relations of one kind or another with their diocesan bishops.
The bishops have generally not been able to reciprocate,
largely because there is no recognized place in the Roman
Catholic Church for units of this kind. They are not
parishes in the usual sense, and they are not religious
orders. They desire a relationship to the whole body, but
not a channel of authoritative direction. On the Protestant
side, the lines are not so clearly drawn. It is possible for
parishes to include communities that resemble the underground in form within their normal structures, and,
indeed, for groups whose outlook and disposition are
identical with those of the underground to have
what amounts to parish status of their own if they desire it.

In general, however, the question of schism has been
avoided as much by the underground's antipathy to becoming organized as by anything else. One observer has described the underground not as *anti*structural but as *pre*-
structural. "Whatever structures exist are conceived as
'functional,' i.e., as serving the purposes of the community
or as derived from the community; however they have to
be checked, for once structures develop a dynamic of their
own they are likely to harm the community rather than to

help it."[18] As long as this is the case, the question of institutional separation is hardly relevant. Any formal separatist step would be a denial of the underground's basic stance. But if, in order to pursue its reforming enthusiasm, the underground begins to acquire some organization, however functional, and if, as a result, it begins to "surface," the picture could rapidly become different. Both representatives of the underground and those of the traditional church organizations would then have to decide how far this organizational trend should be allowed to have separatist overtones. Such are the dilemmas of institutionalization that the underground might have difficulty avoiding the fate of becoming one more denomination.

Meanwhile the underground's prestructural stance can be maintained, in part, because it borrows patterns of social cohesion from society at large. The studies of the sociologist Rocco Caporale, conducted in the United States, France, and Chile, show that most members of underground communities are homogeneous in terms of level of education and social status. College educated, professionally employed, socially and geographically mobile, these are precisely the sorts of persons, particularly in Roman Catholicism, for whom the traditional parish structure and indeed their whole religious identity is in question. They need to find similar persons with whom to share their dilemmas. Very often the resulting communities are composed of persons who already know each other on a neighborhood or professional basis. There is a strong tendency under such conditions for the underground community to be a kind of socially preprogrammed ingroup, lacking the diversity that can exist, ironically, in the traditional parish. Indeed several underground gatherings in large cities have been discovered to represent the social and economic upper class, to celebrate the Sacrament around tables set with the finest china and silver in settings complete with butlers and maids!

Whatever the composition and style of the group, the younger generation, those under twenty-five, are strikingly absent and apparently uninterested. Their alienation from the institutional church apparently has a different character. They do not have to struggle so hard to be free of parish patterns, and they seek community in ways that make less use of explicit eucharistic symbolism.[19]

One can easily, and correctly, infer that the underground communities experience strong pressure toward introversion and self-concern. Gathered because they share a common identity problem, members of some groups too soon begin to concentrate their attentions on themselves. The social concerns that initially loomed so large recede into the background. But Father Caporale makes the interesting observation that ecumenically constructed groups, those composed of both Protestants and Catholics, resist this tendency better than those of only one church background. Possibly this is because members of ecumenical groups find their different identity problems as hard to reconcile as their original forms of churchmanship! They then have greater incentive to find solutions in the worldly setting that they have already experienced and must continue to wrestle with together. In such gatherings there is less interest in exploring the meanings of liturgy per se and more in setting liturgy in relation to theological and ethical concerns, often with a high degree of freedom and innovation.

Is the underground a model for the church of the future? Some suspect that it is. If visible church institutions crumble, underground communities could persist. But only if they succeed in becoming not merely communities for those having identity difficulties with the traditional churches, but also communities for those with a coherent Christian ethical and theological stance indigenous to the contemporary world.

5. The Task-oriented Ministry

A form of ecumenical experiment with unique characteristics of its own is now emerging in metropolitan areas, particularly where the church seeks to minister to particular social needs or to distinct social groups. "The task-oriented ministry" is as good a label as any because this form generally originates in the work of a few individuals who devote themselves to meeting a particular need. A community of common concern then gathers around the core ministry, and a much larger company of people find themselves related to the enterprise in varying ways. Acts of worship may involve only the committed and active few, but they may also be extended to the larger group who have little or no sense of "church membership" in the traditional sense, but who are aware of their human implication in the ministry-defining task.

A wide range of examples might be chosen for comment, ranging from formerly traditional congregations and parishes that have found this orientation a basis for renewal, to ministries of the "underground church" type, to communities with a monastic or semimonastic flavor. Task-oriented ministries are also sometimes extensions of, or special groups within, conventional church forms. Attention is given here, however, mainly to ministries of this kind which are independent enterprises. Two examples suffice to illustrate the type.

a. *The Free Church of Berkeley*

The Free Church of Berkeley, California,[20] had its origin in the concern of a group of ministers, Telegraph Avenue merchants, a University of California representative, and several interested onlookers from the hippie community, for the human implications of an expected inundation of the area by youngsters in search of intense personal experience in the summer of 1967. Knowing that many of these pilgrims, like those in the Haight-Ashbury district of San Francisco, faced more emptiness than fulfillment, this diverse group determined to find some way of moving beyond ignorance and hostility to the hippies, some way of ministering to them as human beings. Clearly there would be great need for the necessities of existence: food, clothing, and shelter. Many would suffer the ravages of drugs without help or comfort. "In short," wrote Robert A. McKenzie, one of the original group, "we were aware that there were many hungry, tired, lonely, sick strangers within our gates for whom most of the community had only scorn."

The device chosen was to find a "street" minister who could identify as fully as possible with the hippie community. Richard York, a young Episcopalian just graduated from the Church Divinity School of the Pacific, was hired with Presbyterian financial support and took up residence in an abandoned house just off Telegraph Avenue. There was no thought at this point of founding anything resembling a "church." But there gradually formed a Christian community of hippies oriented to the task of service in the community which called itself the Free Church. Soon this group began to do more than serve. The need for prayer and celebration soon made itself felt.

Around this central worshiping and ministering community a wider community of celebration has gathered. A Christian festival in honor of the Virgin Mary held in the First Presbyterian Church parking lot attracted one thousand people and was marked by rock bands, incense, beads and crosses, prayers, the distribution of New Testaments, as well as by the eucharistic symbols of the blessing of bread and the washing of the hippie feet by the clergy in liturgical dress. A second event, at the Newman Center, honored Francis of Assisi. The ordination of Richard York to the priesthood of the Episcopal Church in March, 1968, offers fascinating insight into the way one diocese confronted the question of integrating such a ministry, symbolically at least, into its work. The people of the hippie community were determined to have a part in this happening. The service in St. Mark's Church proceeded according to the Episcopal order, but with what color and what participation! People of all affiliations from church dignitaries to avowed agnostics, a rock band, the hippie community with crosses and banners and other symbols, many handmade for the occasion. As the procession moved forward, the assembly rose to its feet. Some groups burned incense, others blew colored bubbles and balloons into the air.

A sermon by Dr. John Pairman Brown, of the Church Divinity School, stressed the analogies between Palestinian politics in Jesus' time and the issues of human freedom and dignity today. Jesus was a child of the Galilean resistance, but he rejected its tactics and goals in favor of a "revolutionary nonviolence." Yet he stuck to the end to its cry against injustice. Dr. Brown said he was not alone in having lost interest in the things the denominations once differed on, or in rejecting what they now seemed to agree about: connivance with the American establishment. The grass-roots church was really here, reunion was now happening in this asphalt gathering! Yet the new priest should not identify with the hippie community so completely that he had nothing of his own to offer it.

After the ordination proper came a "free church intercession and litany of the saints" and a service of Holy Communion with an invitation to all eligible to receive Communion in their own churches whatever these might be "since the holy table is the Lord's." Thus Richard York's task-oriented ministry gathered a company of people that transformed the Episcopal liturgy and opened it to an ecumenical world. In turn the worship of the Free Church has become more explicitly eucharistic and has begun to articulate its own ecumenical discipline.

With Richard York's ordination has come a gradual shift toward stress on the "church" side of the Free Church. A worshiping community of from two to five hundred people now meets regularly, and two more ministers, Anthony Nugent, a Presbyterian, and John Pairman Brown, who preached the ordination sermon, have been added to the staff. The specifically hippie element in the Free Church's constituency has somewhat receded. What this congregation now has in common is its political posture, its commitment to disaffiliation from establishment-oriented attitudes and enterprises. This general attitude is shared by a variety of groups within the congregation concerned with a wide range of tasks: the peace movement, the poor, the question of the Berkeley "peoples' park." The most recent project has been the formation of a youth congregation drawn from among the "street people" of the area.

The definition of membership in the Free Church is involvement. In effect, this is an ecumenical congregation practicing open Communion, asking few, if any, questions about other or previous church affiliation, holding a highly politicized and action-oriented view of the Sacraments, and having its own unique liturgies. It is not quite clear what happens, or what ought to happen, when a participant in the Free Church leaves the area and tries to join another Christian body. Yet the leadership is solidly against the idea that to be in the Free Church is to have "dropped out" of the church at large. On the contrary, an effort is made to be in touch with the existing denominations, to have a vote, as it were, to try to "melt the organized churches from the bottom up." And, conversely, the Free Church continues to have financial support from both Episcopalian and Presbyterian sources. Thus the question of being "in communion" with these bodies is raised in new and highly pragmatic ways.

b. *Emmaus House, New York City*

Emmaus House,[21] a radical Christian community in New York City, shares characteristics both of the task-oriented ministry and of the underground church. The classification, of course, matters little. Emmaus House is discussed in this section rather than in the last mainly because, like the Free Church of Berkeley, it is more than a house congregation. It has a degree of official church sponsorship, clerical leadership, and a home of its own. It is oriented to definite ministerial tasks. It acquires its following, and, indeed, builds its worshiping community, from among persons who wish to share these particular commitments from a Christian perspective.

Emmaus House is the work of two young priests, David Kirk and Lyle Young, who met in Rome while the former was studying at the Beda College. Father Kirk, among other things, was a correspondent for *The Catholic World* and the *Catholic Worker*. With his press card he attended all the press conferences of the Vatican Council, and here, he claims, he learned most of his theology. Already a Catholic of the Melkite rite (he had joined a Melkite church during his student days in Mississippi because it seemed less rigid, more open), Father Kirk was ordained a Melkite priest in Jerusalem in 1964. Father Young, with a rather rich background as Catholic turned Anglican and again turned Catholic, was at the time of this writing awaiting transfer to the Melkite rite as well, along with Father Richard Mann, a priest of strong artistic bent, who subsequently joined the Emmaus staff.

This background of the guiding spirits of the Emmaus community is important because it indicates a number of strands of influence important for grasping the flavor of this enterprise. Apart from the personal experiences of all three priests with ecclesiastical rigidity and with the plight of the poor, Father Kirk's connection with the Catholic "new left" through the "Catholic Worker" movement and his status as a Melkite priest do much to explain the orientation of Emmaus House and how it operates. The first affiliation is the root of Father Kirk's conviction that political concern lies at the heart of the gospel; the second offers him the freedom to put these convictions into action.

The Melkite rite, an Eastern Catholic body in communion with but not under the administrative direction of Rome, has about fifty-five thousand adherents in the United States, most of Egyptian and other Arabic backgrounds. It seems also to be the most radical and open wing of Catholicism. Melkite bishops have consistently expressed views on divorce, birth control, liturgy, and social action well to the left of those of Roman prelates. For Father Kirk, his tie to the American bishop of the Melkite rite offers him freedom from the more conservative administration of Cardinal Cooke in New York.

Emmaus House is obviously many things. The concerns of its priests and lay participants range from antiwar protest and draft resistance to the immediate needs of the poor, particularly those of the black community. Beyond the specifics, Emmaus is concerned with what might be called the re-formation of the church in a new social stance with a new spirit of openness with a newly participatory style of life.

Celebrations of Communion in this community resemble those of the typical underground house church with perhaps a little more elaboration. The worshiping community includes many non-Catholics. The Liturgy of the Word, that part of the service before the Mass proper, is prepared each week by different members of the congregation. Often centered around a particular theme, the liturgy may include announcements of activities in which participants are involved, readings from a variety of sources, spontaneous remarks by members of the group, silent meditation. The Communion itself is with baskets of bread and

CHRISTIAN CELEBRATION IN THE WORLD 79

chalices of wine received standing, crowded around the dining room table, to the tune of the song chosen for the day.

Repeatedly, one hears in these celebrations the theme of rebirth, rebirth of the self, rebirth of the church. The meaning is that one must be born again out of self-interest and self-concern to perceive the sacramental realities that happen in the world. A revolution is incipient in this rebirth, not a violent upheaval but an active rejection of existing institutions and value systems to clear the ground for a new conception of society. So far as the church organization is concerned, this means resistance to arbitrary authority, a "faithful disobedience" growing out of "faithfulness to the church as it ought to be." It is not a question of doing away with structures altogether, but rather a matter of seeing authority "radically redefined as a democratic, coordinating, tying together force, rather than an infallible, didactic one." Father Kirk likes to quote Cardinal Newman: "The *community* is the authority; the voice of God is in the *people.*"

The worshiping community at Emmaus House is constituted in just this way. To participate in the ministry is to participate in the Communion celebration, whatever one's formal church affiliation may be, or even if one has none. For Father Young, "the Church is, first and above all, the community of mankind and not the community of the baptized." Or in Father Kirk's words: "We believe that we must share Communion with other faiths before any dogmatic definition of the Presence has been reached. . . . You know the story of Emmaus: some disciples met a stranger on the road but didn't recognize him as Jesus resurrected until they had broken bread together. In the early Church, the differences of opinion about the nature of the Eucharist were infinitely more violent than they are now between Protestants and Catholics, and yet *they* were sharing Communion."

6. ECUMENICAL MARRIAGES

Marriages between Christians of different confessions have not always been seen as ecumenical opportunities. Until very recently, the pastoral advice given by most churches has consisted of warnings against the dangers of mixed marriages. More positive attitudes have been reserved for cases in which the union across confessional lines was clearly inevitable, and even then have taken the form and tone of reluctant concessions, in some cases with legal conditions attached.

But contrast this with the striking new statement of the Ecumenical Commission of the Archdiocese of Boston dated May, 1969:

> Ecumenical marriages should be treated as normal in our society, and the parties should be made to feel that in such a union deeply religious lives are possible for them. There is a need today for pastors to see and to stress the positive aspects of the marriage and to help the couple to formulate attitudes that will enable their marriage to be a true ecumenical encounter in which they can make a real contribution to the work of Christian unity. "In fact, such marriages contain the possibility of becoming a prophetic sign of the triumph of the love of the Lord over the division of the churches."[22]

Clearly a vision now exists in which the ecumenical marriage is as much a new form of Christian gathering in the contemporary world as any of the other experiments just recounted. The grounds for saying this are, of course, not new. What is new is the recognition of the significance of these grounds both by certain couples and by some church authorities.

The basis for seeing marriage as a form of the church lies, of course in several perspectives to be found in the Bible. The male-female relationship is recognized in Gen. 1:27 as not only a basic structure of creation but also as one of those features of human life involved in the idea of being "in the image of God." Not just sexual duality is meant here, but mutuality, dialogue, the possibility of deeply human interaction. And the New Testament takes up this theme in Eph., ch. 5. There the relation between husband and wife is compared to the relation of Christ to his church. Thus at the very least a marriage can be a community visibly embodying God's covenant intention toward man; in short, it can be a churchly reality in a certain sense.

Through most of Christian history the assumption has been that a marriage could fulfill this possibility not in its own right but by being begun and lived out within some larger confessional community, Roman Catholic, Orthodox, Protestant. Thus the horror of mixed marriages. In a divided Christendom, the mixed marriage simply went beyond what church authorities could recognize as churchly reality, and hence it became a legalistic battleground instead of an ecumenical opportunity. Today's pluralistic, mobile culture, however, changes all this. An increasingly high proportion of marriages are mixed, and this of course includes the combination of different faiths and of faith with no faith at all, as well as unions of Christians from different churches.

The denominational traditions that we now have are no more prepared to speak with a common voice about what an ecumenical marriage really is than they are to agree about Communion services that cross, or ignore, their boundaries. There is, however, a new will to work on this question. Is any Christian marriage a sacrament, for example, and if it is, who makes it so, the officiating clergyman or the couple themselves? The Orthodox tradition insists that the priest brings the sacramental character to the marriage rite, while Roman Catholicism teaches that the sacrament is actually performed by the couple, provided that they marry in fellowship with the church. In fact, the priest needs to be present only for reasons of church discipline. For the Protestant churches, marriage is not counted as one of the formal sacraments, although its sacramental character is increasingly widely recognized.

In all the churches, moreover, there are anomalies in the relationships between theological teaching and actual practice. The requirements of the different church disciplines partly reflect their theological positions and partly reflect accidental historical circumstances. This is particularly true of regulations covering divorce, annulment, and remarriage, as well as of relations with the civil authorities and with each other.[23]

Several practices, which might have been thought revolutionary a mere five years ago, are now becoming increasingly common. The general improvement in atmosphere between Protestants and Roman Catholics that has come as a result of joint ecumenical effort now opens the way for many forms of practical pastoral cooperation. Priests are encouraged to be in touch with Protestant ministers in their areas, to be familiar with the marriage regulations of Protestant churches, and to be in touch when a mixed marriage is proposed. No longer is the idea to be automatically discouraged. Rather, the way otherwise being clear, the opportunities and responsibilities of such a relationship are to be pointed out. Premarital instruction may now be jointly given. And if the marriage occurs in a Roman Catholic church, many dioceses now permit the priest to invite the Protestant minister to take part in the ceremony. Most often this would involve prayers and blessings rather than actual pronouncement of the marriage, but the matter is left open.[24]

Beyond this, there are possibilities now available by special dispensation. In 1966, an American Presbyterian girl engaged to an Italian Roman Catholic received permission from Vatican authorities to receive Communion at the nuptial Mass celebrated according to the Roman rite.[25] The priest in charge, a chaplain attached to the Catholic

Action movement in the Italian universities, married the couple in Assisi on September 21 of that year. Certain requirements were imposed upon the Protestant bride: that she formally declare her faith in the "real presence" of Christ in the Eucharist and that she acknowledge that the validity of Roman Catholic sacraments is tied to the structure of that church, which in turn is grounded on the authority of the Pope. With this precedent, the Roman Catholic bishops of the Netherlands announced in March, 1968, that the non-Catholic partner in a marriage might, on request to the bishop with jurisdiction, receive Communion at the nuptial Mass.[26] The Dutch bishops imposed a somewhat different set of conditions. The non-Catholic must be baptized, be in general harmony with the Roman Catholic faith as it is expressed in the Mass, and be in good standing in his own church. The last requirement is a wise one from the ecumenical point of view, recognizing as it does the disciplines of non-Roman Catholic bodies. By 1969, the Boston Archdiocese was offering the same possibility, at the discretion of the Cardinal, if the non-Catholic was "well informed and properly disposed."[27]

A second broad possibility has now begun to open that a Protestant-Roman Catholic marriage may take place before a Protestant minister either in a Roman Catholic or in a Protestant church. This normally requires dispensation from Rome, but, the dispensation given, the Catholic priest is then free to participate in the ceremony as well. No special requirements are apparently laid down as to the content of the rite. An excellent example of such a ceremony was recorded in the *National Catholic Reporter* for April 3, 1968.[28] A Roman Catholic bride wrote her own wedding liturgy for her marriage to a Quaker in the Quaker chapel at Antioch College, Yellow Springs, Ohio. The liturgy combined elements of both Catholic and Quaker traditions, and a Catholic priest, the Quaker vice-president of the College, and a Methodist chaplain all took part in the service. The two former recited in unison that, as the couple "have made these faithful promises before this company and have sanctified them by giving and receiving rings, we rejoice to recognize them as husband and wife together." The Archbishop of Cincinnati had given permission for the form of the liturgy to be worked out in consultation with the local parish priest.

The vexed issue of promises regarding the education of children can now also be eased by seeking dispensations, which are more easily granted than was formerly the case. If the non-Catholic party cannot make the customary promises, either orally or in writing, dispensation may be sought provided no prior agreement has been made that would exclude the possibility of raising the children in the Catholic faith, and provided that the Roman Catholic partner accepts the responsibility to raise the children as Catholics if possible.

By granting permissions and dispensations, the Roman Catholic Church has moved farther toward the recognition of new ecumenical realities in the area of mixed marriage than in other realms of ecumenical relationship. Yet the *Instruction* of March 18, 1966, still the official policy statement on the subject, is not nearly so open on these matters as present practice in many dioceses would suggest. The problems of dogma and discipline mentioned earlier have not been solved, and the *Instruction* reflects this fact. But Roman Catholic authorities, where marriage is concerned, are acknowledging in practical ways that the Christian reality can exist in ecumenical form beyond their dogma and discipline. Could this be a model for further ecumenical progress? Could it be that many apparent problems will not be "solved" at all, but rather rendered obsolete by contextually sensitive pastoral action?

Whatever concessions and innovations may be made to facilitate ecumenical marriage *ceremonies,* the question remains whether there are truly such things as ecumenical *marriages.* The case studies really needed here would have to delve into the quality and meaning of family life in ecumenical households, and into the relation to all this of Christian symbols and meanings. So long as the churches are divided, mixed marriages will continue to be in an ecclesiastical no-man's-land. Pastoral care for such couples ought to be a common task for Christian churches, one in which the good of the family and not rival claims ought to be foremost.

It would seem that in all too few mixed marriages do the partners receive much relevant guidance about what the potentialities of their relationship might be. They go to one or the other church, or to none at all. There are few knowledgeably supportive communities in which they could begin to work out an ecumenical style of Christian family life. While no one should want to turn a personal relationship into a theological laboratory, it is obvious that no one knows enough about what goes on in these unions and that not enough systematic data has been gathered to be of significant help. In theory, the ecumenical marriage should teach us more about the churches' future than any other transconfessional venture. But this is because marriage raises, in acute form, all the problems of indigenizing ancient institutions in the modern world. Married couples cannot insulate themselves from reality the way church institutions can and do. If Christian marriages are authentic forms of Christian gathering, how do they actually go about being so in the midst of a secularized culture? The existence of ecumenical marriage ceremonies and of ecumenical pastoral care is a precondition for answering this question, but not the answer itself.

7. Some Tentative Observations

The experiments described in this chapter are representative of many more that could have been treated.

Moreover, the descriptions themselves merely skim the surface. It has seemed better to give an impression of the range and diversity of experimentation than to attempt exhaustive analyses. The latter, of course, ought to be done, with research models designed to find out what has happened to the outlook of the experimenters and others. We would like to know, in short, whether any of these new instances and forms of eucharistic community are changing the church in a measurable way. Do people find themselves transformed by their contact with these communities? If so, how and why?

Enough information is available here, however, to allow some tentative comments. The first concerns what the experimentalists are basically trying to do. The second has to do with how one might arrive at relevant criteria for judging their success.

There is litle doubt, first, that the basic intention is to do "what the church does." The forms of worship and their congregational contexts here are recognizably eucharistic. While established church authorities very often decline to recognize the experiments as ecclesial in terms of given institutional definitions, there is no inclination on anyone's part to call these efforts unchristian or to label them as false worship. The intention to celebrate the traditional Christian Sacrament is obvious. Thus the gatherings described here are to be distinguished from the vast array of other sorts of community experiments, some of them loosely related to the church, which do not have this intention. Sensitivity groups, gatherings for group therapy, and the like, do not claim to be forms of the church in the way these experiments do.

Along with this is the fact that the forms of eucharistic worship that one finds in the experiments are relatively free of innovation for innovation's sake. What innovations there are turn out to be in the interest of directness and simplicity, with much interest in the use of ancient forms such as the Liturgy of Hippolytus. Contemporary music and situation-oriented prayer find their place, but seldom do such elements threaten to make the basic liturgy unrecognizable. The most common innovation is simply the incorporation of the Eucharist with a common meal. One is struck by the fact that the genuinely bizarre and "far out" transformations of the Sacrament are often found in contexts that are not really experimental at all: rather, some pastor or chaplain is trying to shore up attendance at his traditional service in his traditional Gothic sanctuary. As a rule the more genuinely immersed in the world an act of Holy Communion is, the more confronted by danger and the more prepared to give of itself the community is, the simpler and more direct will be its liturgy.

The liturgical modifications found in experimental contexts are simply contextually determined. Thus, if the context is a house, the Sacrament will be around a table. And if the surroundings are natural, it will be natural also for everyone present to participate, whatever their relations may be to the church at large. Closed Communion may seem appropriate where the surroundings are remote and mysterious, but not where the sacramental forms are basically those of common human life. Thus it seems to follow that if one is serious about moving the Sacrament to a *social* location outside the sanctuary, certain changes in both practice and theological attitudes are bound to follow. There will be an attempted indigenization of both forms and meanings. But this will not mean that the celebration is any less an expression of the integral Christian intention.

The real issue, however, is not just what is intended but also what is achieved. Do any of these experiments succeed in finding forms of Christian celebration that are at home in the contemporary world? Are any indigenous not just in the sense that they have accommodated themselves to the expectations of modern culture but also in the sense that they have made the distinctiveness of Biblical faith evident in terms this culture can understand? Do any, in fact, break through to a new model for Communion not only as liturgy but also as style of life? Or do they represent only a series of ingenious variants on the old models, subsisting, with effort, in some interesting places but destined, sooner or later, to go the way of all such anachronisms? Such questions are hard to answer. We are not sure we would recognize an authentic new model if we saw it!

Thus a more modest question comes first. What do the experimenters think the theological *criterion* of indigenization ought to be? The logic of what is said and done in most of these cases involves one form or another of the insight of Paul Ricoeur at the Pentecost Eucharist in Paris. The world, seen as an arena in which new manifestations of humanity are bursting forth and striving with the old political and ideological powers, becomes the common ground between the Christians drawn together in these celebrations. As Ricoeur says, the workers and students were "third parties" between the Catholic and Protestant churchmen. These human beings, not involved in the institutional church, brought the different Christian confessions together. Their presence, according to Ricoeur, was to be compared with the presence of the bread and wine. They were the link, the bridge, between otherwise separated Christians.

Some such idea seems implicit in most of the experiments. In some cases the "world" is literally present at an act of Communion. This was true, for example, at the ordination of the priest of the Free Church of Berkeley, Richard York. In other cases, the Pentecost Eucharist for instance, the world was present in the politically pregnant occasion of the celebration, as well as in the well-proved personal commitments of the participants. In still other cases, house churches and mixed marriages among them, Communion has a worldly setting because the people present *are* the world and celebrate the feast in ways that are symbolically congruent with ordinary life. And even where the surroundings are more or less ecclesiastical, with bishops, church executives, priests, nuns, and Student Christian Movement officers as far as the eye can see, the subject matter under discussion and the commitments generated or reaffirmed can provide a worldly context if honesty and realism are the notes of the occasion. In all these cases the will to make the Eucharist meaningful in the "situation" is the factor that determines its outward form and, indeed, strongly conditions the understanding of Christian community, the "ecclesiology," associated with it. In most such cases it is impossible to "fence the table" according to existing church rules if real indigenization is to be maintained. Indeed, the line between "church" and "world" becomes as indefinite as the lines between churches.

This line of argument does not identify the worldly presence of God in Christ with revolution or humanization *tout court*. It rather seems to find that presence at the point where Christians, under the compulsion of the gospel, find that they can become creatively involved in the world's struggles, and hence have a presence to celebrate. To put it another way, the presence of Christ is identified where the tradition, in the hands of involved Christians, meets the human reality with which it is concerned. This meeting is marked by a rush of ecstatic recognition. It becomes the moment for celebration. Thus the objective evidence of Christ's presence in the world *is* the presence there of eucharistic community. It is not something that can be argued on an objective basis from the general characteristics of the secular or in other similar ways. The presence of Christ in the secular environment is a presence "in, with, and under" outward structures and events. It is detected not by dispassionate analysis but by personal involvement, which, with the recognition of the brother, can become eucharistic.

The accent here is upon meeting, upon living inter-action. It is impossible, from this perspective, to see how the New Testament promise can be present *either* in the organized churches with their tradition *or* in·the world if these two are taken separately. Traditionalists tend to con-centrate on one locus, activist radicals on the other. Their problems are equally insoluble. The churches are indeed formal guardians of the message, but are they the social reality among men to which the message points? The world may be full of revolutionary new happenings, but does history, in itself, offer men a sense of direction? The presence we seek occurs in a juncture between the two that takes eucharistic form.

The danger is that men who have lived out such a meeting will tend to absolutize and forever hold on to the particular form it took. Worse, people who never experi-enced the original meeting with its liberating ecstasy may look for salvation in the form alone. They may cultivate it and rationalize it and become preoccupied with its internal workings. They may, in fact, believe that they are doing something revolutionary when they are not. One can never be sure that one is not seeing a group of Christians, alienated from church and world for special reasons of their own, meeting to celebrate their own togetherness.

If this happens, both the Christian tradition and the world's agony are being exploited for the purpose of making a small group feel relevant, while this relevance remains to be proved in the course of events. The claim of experi-mental communities to represent the authentic Christian intention must be respected, but these communities are not the only ones entitled to judge how faithful their version of the Christian intention is. Similarly, the claim that the human struggle is really reflected in the community's political involvements should be heard, but other men, outside the church, whose struggle this is, may also have something to say.

Thus listening to the rationale of what experimental communities have done is not enough. One must listen to a great deal else besides and try to discern what is authentic. Apart from praying and hoping for the discerning Spirit, the most helpful thing one can do is to seek the perspective of past attempts at indigenization. This the next chapter sets out to do.

CHAPTER III

A Contextual Look
at the Churches

It is an ecumenical fact that Christians, separated from one another by church traditions, are discovering the possibility of new kinds of worshiping community where they meet in the life of the world. These discoveries are sometimes shared by persons who are otherwise alienated from the churches altogether. A new kind of communion seems to be in the making, a kind of celebratory gathering that not only breaks existing church rules but comes into being in social and political contexts from which the organized churches are largely absent.

How are such gatherings related to existing Christian traditions? Some say that the experience of the churches is too tainted by ideological compromise and institutional self-interest to be of much use. But if this is so, what is to prevent the experimenters from sooner or later stumbling in the same ways? A study of existing church positions is important for even the most far-out ecumenical experimenters for at least two reasons.

First, whatever their degree of obedience or relevance, the churches have been transmitters into the modern world of the word of expectation on which ecumenical experiments are based. They have some knowledge of the difficulties of translating this word into social reality. The vast majority of the experimenters were, in fact, brought up in the churches, and there first heard the message of expectation and promise that they are now trying to live in new ways. Thus the churches represent previous attempts to indigenize the gospel. Some of the most obviously anachronistic elements in existing traditions are evidence of success in this indigenization effort at other places and times.

Second, the churches as we know them are the only *universal* expression of Christianity in concrete form. However imperfect this universality may be, it remains true that the organized churches represent a form in which Christian faith is known around the globe. They and their agencies are a medium of communication between Christians. Their interrelated theological products are a basis for self-understanding, a common language for Christian gatherings. Only by being in touch with some wider Christian reality can the different experimental communities avoid a certain kind of parochialism and narrowness that denies the "catholic" character of Christian faith. Today's experimenters, if they fell into isolation, could reproduce some of the same half-truths that have divided the church before. They could repeat the blunders that have turned the search for authenticity and freedom into defensiveness and narrowness. They could echo the uncritical worldliness that has turned the search for relevance into compromise and accommodation. Not to speak of the danger of creating new divisions as needless and pointless as some in the past.

But if the churches have all this experience and wisdom, why are they still so divided and disobedient? There is obviously a difference between learning what the past has to teach, which anybody ought to be willing to do, and binding oneself to the past's products, which may be quite another matter. The ecumenical movement has created a situation in which increasing numbers of Christians are able to view their denominational histories with trans-denominational insight. This new awareness has had some

unexpected results. For some, it has produced a drive
toward universal churchly unity. For others, it has raised a
question: If each denomination is the historically condi-
tioned product of its time, can one escape these limitations
by putting them all together? May it not be that what the
churches have in common, when we finally express it, will
turn out to be as historically relative as the things that keep
them apart? May it not be that the basic image of the
church being pursued by the organized ecumenical movement is a time-conditioned artifact? If these things are
true, then an authentic Christian gathering today will have
to be of a new *kind,* not just a unified version of the old
kind.

The vision of the nature of Christian community with
which the ecumenical movement has been working still
relies in part upon assumptions that come from the "Constantinian" period of church history. By now, of course,
the idea of a "Constantinian" churchmanship is common-
place among theologians. The term refers to the great
change that took place when, in A.D. 313, the Emperor
Constantine launched the process that made Christianity
the dominant Roman religion, and to the long-term consequences of that move. In a word, from that time until very
recently Christianity has been in various ways the official
religious expression of the societies in which it has developed, a fact that has profoundly influenced our understanding of the content of the faith itself. The church has
been, in one way or another, a visible, public institution:
an organization. So much so that it is difficult now to
imagine it in any other way. And this has been more than
a matter of security, wealth, and privilege, as if these
factors were not sufficiently corrupting in themselves. The
"Constantinian" arrangement has decisively shaped Christian theological concepts and moral precepts. While the
importance of what the emperor did is widely appreciated,
the penetration of the consequences into virtually every

twist and turn of Christian thought is only now beginning to be thoroughly understood.

The key concept needed for such an understanding is not at all foreign to Christian habits of reflection. This faith has insisted from the beginning that the Christian reality is met in gathering, that theology is the product of an interchange of community insight. Today a discipline known as "sociology of knowledge" is saying much the same thing: that what we take to be "reality" is a community product; that a given society will have certain habits of thought which it will take for granted, while in fact the nature of these conceptualizations will depend on the kind of society it is. We express truth in words and symbols, and these words and symbols are products of our past which we now share and shape together with our fellow human beings. What we are as a society will be revealed in the way we think. Thus the thinking of the church will reveal what *it* is as a community. *Its* experience in history, *its* moral commitments, *its* triumphs and failures will build up a background for *its* thought. Moreover the church will not depend wholly on ideas of its own. There will be an interaction between what the church is as a society and the broader society within which it exists. What that society thinks of the church will have its effect, as well as what church thinks of society in return.

Many attempts have been made to track down these connections with some precision. One of the most suggestive is a study by Guy E. Swanson, a sociologist at the University of California at Berkeley, entitled *Religion and Regime.*[29] Swanson's work is not a substitute for histories of dogma of the more familiar type, but the implications of his study deserve close attention. Swanson has examined the relations between structures of Christian thought and the political systems in some forty-one independent political units in Europe at the time of the Reformation. The purpose has been to discover correlations, if any exist,

between the regimes by which these societies were gov-
erned and the religious choices they made at the time of
their "Reformation settlements," when decisions were
made to be officially Roman Catholic or Protestant, and, if
Protestant, what brand of Protestantism to embrace.

Swanson classifies "religions" and "regimes" in terms of
the degree to which they see governing power as "im-
manent" in the institutions and symbols with which this
power is related. A high degree of immanence means that
the institution or symbol is virtually identified with the
power behind it and largely devoid of any identity of its
own. Politically, a highly immanental regime would be one
in which every social institution was conceived as a direct
expression of the ruler's personality and will, as in an
absolute monarchy. Religiously, an immanental system
would be one in which divine power was considered to
inhere directly in religious objects, persons, or symbols: in
which there was conceived to be a one-to-one correspon-
dence between the authority of religious institution and
the higher authority it was believed to represent.

"Religions" and "regimes" in Swanson's classification are
then less immanental as the distance grows greater between
the sources of ultimate authority and the visible instru-
ments related to them. Politically, a regime with a low
degree of immanence would be one in which political decisions were made by the interaction of separate organized
power interests, none of them identified with the regime
as a whole. Confidence would be placed in the rationality
of the interactive process producing both conflict and agreement. The ultimate sovereignty would not be considered
inherent in any political person, institution, or symbol,
but would somehow be considered to transcend all these
instrumentalities absolutely. Such a regime might or might
not have a central executive to carry out what amounted to
management functions. Religiously, a system with a low
degree of immanence would correspond to this. No reli-

gious organization or institution, or any person or symbol, would be remotely identified with the divine authority. Considerable confidence might be placed in the human logic of the religious system, intellectually and otherwise. But God would be felt to transcend all this absolutely.

Swanson, of course, pictures a continuum of "religions" and "regimes" between the immanental and nonimmanental extremes. He finds five basic types of political structure in Reformation Europe ranging along this spectrum, from "centralist" regimes on the right through "commensal," "limited centralist," and "balanced" regimes in the center, to "heterarchic" regimes on the left. He finds a very high degree of correlation between the "centralist" and "commensal" regimes and the decision to retain Roman Catholicism, between the "limited centralist" and "balanced" regimes and the decision to adopt Anglicanism or Lutheranism, and between the "heterarchic" regimes and the decision to adopt some version of the Reformed position.

Swanson's book works out the classification of political regimes particularly fully, with close attention to detail and to the application of his concepts to actual political and social conditions. He explores the theological positions involved much less fully. He summarizes the latter in rather static generalities, and afterward is content to label the different Reformation settlements as Anglican, Lutheran, Roman Catholic, or Reformed without further attention to the inner dynamics of these tendencies. Yet his suggestions are worth close attention by both sociologists and theologians.

Swanson draws no long-range conclusions from his analysis, nor does he ask why the relationships are as they appear to be. It does not seem that theology is simply a reflection of politics but rather that religious thought and social structures seem to interact in such a way as to tap a range of images that come naturally to the people of a given culture. These images appear to be deep-seated and very persistent metaphors, built into the cultural contents and language patterns characteristic of the society, which tend to shape typical conceptions of *power* on the one hand and *community* on the other. These conceptions are inevitably interrelated, and there is nothing the society does that they do not touch. Theology and politics play out the same metaphors, and if one wishes to speak of the Christian reality or the lack of it in a given situation, one must do so in terms of the images and the interplay, not in terms of separate organized entities called "church" and "state."

This is probably true for both "Constantinian" and non-"Constantinian" situations. It probably does not matter whether the church legitimates a society's values either in establishment or dissent, or whether it functions as a counterforce to those values. The whole reality with which we have to deal is a complex interaction, not a religious institution. The religious institution is there, but to understand the reality that it and the society bring into being, we need more than what has usually been meant by "ecclesiology" or the "doctrine of the church." We need a sort of analysis that as yet has no name, and probably only exists in rudimentary form.

It does not follow from what has been said that there is no place in this interaction for formative theological criticism. One must remember, of course, that theologians as a class, like other intellectuals, represent a very special segment of the population of any age. They are immersed, by training and study, in a contrasting culture: the Biblical culture. They are steeped in a set of metaphors and images that have certain meanings in their context, a context kept alive within the society of theologians and clerics but largely closed to most other men whether medieval or modern. It is possible for a theologian to try to bring the Word to bear upon the interactions that constitute the social reality of his own age. But he cannot be sure how this Word is going to be heard, if it is heard at all. Communication will not take place unless it is tied to the right symbolic relationships. Whatever the theologian or cleric says will be heard, first of all, in terms of the speaker's social role as society conceives it. And knowledge of his role will, in turn, affect what the speaker says and how he says it.

The extreme subtlety and complexity of this situation makes it easy to understand why the theologians of renewal today have so difficult a time making themselves understood, and why it is so hard for them to find metaphors that can turn what they have to say into imagined social reality. It also explains why the churches have such difficulty trying to *be* the social reality of which the New Testament message speaks. At most, they can only be part of the social interaction out of which such a social reality would have to be constructed.

The "Constantinian" situation is passing out of existence. It is not evident, however, that this makes embodiment of the Word in society more difficult. In some ways it may make it easier by simplifying the symbolic interactions involved in communication. It will be clearer, in the future, whether you are hearing the message or not. At the moment, of course, many features of "Constantinianism" still remain. The ancient religious symbols are still employed by groups that remain in a position to use them for social control. Others find in these symbols profound sources of comfort and reassurance. In neither case is it clear that the New Testament Word is being embodied, although one cannot be sure.

The churches themselves are in a highly complex position. It would seem that every existing Christian body continues today to bear the marks of the metaphors of sovereignty and community that were current at the time and place of its foundation. These metaphors are deeply embedded in the different understandings of Christian truth and of church order with which we have to deal. At the same time, the churches are well aware that they have lived into an era when the social situations in which they were rooted have vanished. The old metaphors no longer come naturally—they have to be defended by theologians. The increasingly recognized relativity of these metaphors has produced the ecumenical movement. The churches move toward one another in the hope that they will find the new metaphor in which the Christian reality can take root in a new time.

There follows a series of sketches, no more, of how this process is working out in the different confessional groups. There is no intention here of writing adequate history. Rather, each confession is treated in what might be termed a documented characterization.

1. THE ORTHODOX CHURCHES

The Eastern Orthodox Churches, today numbering nineteen separate bodies united by common beliefs, customs, and traditions, trace their origin to the Christianity of the Eastern Roman Empire which subsequently became Byzantium. Orthodoxy subsequently spread to other areas, notably medieval Muscovy. Today the Patriarchates of Constantinople and Moscow share world leadership in the Orthodox communion.

Much of the substance of the Orthodox tradition, including the work of the seven Ecumenical Councils which is considered normative for Orthodox faith and practice, is the indirect result of the efforts of Constantine and his successors to establish and maintain the religious unity of the East. The development of doctrine also reflected the rivalry between the various Eastern patriarchal centers, especially Antioch, Alexandria, and Constantinople, with the latter becoming preeminent. After the capture of Constantinople by the Turks in 1453, Russian Orthodoxy rapidly grew in influence.

All these regimes would, in Swanson's classification, be called "centralist." Yet this centralism, as it developed, did not become as legalistic, uniform, and rigid as some Western political institutions tended to be. One might speak, instead, of a kind of decentralized centralism that made much of the traditions of different localities and opened the way for the "autocephalous" (i.e., each with its own head) Orthodox bodies that emerged. In Russia, especially, not merely political institutions but the land itself was felt to be holy. Much of the special quality of the awareness of community in Orthodoxy is to be traced to these beginnings. Clearly a hierarchical system, and certainly believing that Christ is really present in the Sacrament, Orthodoxy has nevertheless evolved neither the notion of church authority nor the elaborate and precise definitions of the manner of Christ's presence in the bread and wine that one finds in Roman Catholic history. Rather an intense sense of community as the integrity of a people has been dominant. And the Eucharist has been seen as completely inseparable from this communal integrity. Either one is part of the community in every way or one is not.

A statement of the 1965 Standing Conference of Canonical Orthodox Bishops puts the consequences of this as follows:

As unworthy inheritors of the faith committed to the Apostles and Fathers by Almighty God, and preserved unsullied in the Church through the centuries, we contribute to the reintegration of Christendom by witnessing to the precious confession delivered to us, more especially as it relates to the Eucharist, the Sacrament or Mystery of unity. It is, as all of her faithful children are aware, the ancient, unvarying, and unalterable teaching of the Orthodox Church that the reception of Holy Communion is the final end and goal of the Chris-

tian life, the very fulfillment of unity. It is the last step in that
earthly Christian progress which unites the faithful to Christ
the Lord and to each other in Him. To the Holy Communion
the Church admits only her baptized and chrismated children
who confess the full Orthodox faith, pure and entire, and by it
she shows forth their oneness with her and with her Divine
Spouse. Holy Communion is the sign and evidence of right
belief and of the incorporation in the Israel of God. Further,
the Church teaches that the Eucharist cannot be found, and
must not be sought, outside of her covenanted mysteries. It is
the achievement of unity.

The Standing Conference would at this time remind the
children of the Church as they pray, study and work for
Christian reunion, that the Eucharistic Mystery is the end of
unity, not a means to that end, and that therefore, decisions
regarding Holy Communion reached by Christian bodies outside of the Orthodox Church have no significance or validity
for the Orthodox Church or her members. Holy Communion
will not be sought by Orthodox Christians outside of the
Church, nor will it be offered to those who do not yet confess
the Orthodox Church as their mother.[30]

This general position has since been reaffirmed in
several more recent statements by the Patriarch of Constantinople, Athenagoras. The Patriarch's letter of March
14, 1967, addressed to Archbishop Iakovos of North and
South America, for example, seeks to correct the impression
that moves toward greater cordiality between Orthodox and
Roman Catholics mean that the issue of *communicatio in
sacris* is thereby solved. "Inter-communion between the
Orthodox and other churches," the Patriarch writes, "does
not as yet exist."[31]

The considerations underlying this viewpoint have been
the subject of much debate among individual Orthodox
theologians. No one opinion has become official. This is
characteristic of Orthodoxy. The Orthodox churches are
what they are by tradition, by actual life, and not by application of verbalized theological principles. Observers from

the Western world must be particularly careful not to assume that thought categories, which come from outside the Orthodox world, can be immediately applied. But perhaps the most illuminating discussion of the Orthodox attitude (in this case as it applies to Roman Catholicism) is to be found in a paper written in 1967 by Msgr. Myles Bourke and Archpriest John Meyendorff for an Orthodox–Roman Catholic consultation.[32] The Orthodox attitude "is determined by the conviction that participation in the sacraments of the Church involves total commitment to the fullness of truth received in Jesus Christ, and that such a commitment is obviously possible only inside the body of the one Church of God." In other words, the important question is whether you are really, fully, part of the church. If you are, you are "in communion." And, if so, such questions as the "validity" of this or that ministry, or the extent to which you are in doctrinal agreement with this or that authority, become relatively unimportant. Ministry and doctrine, at least, do not count as criteria taken in the abstract, in isolation from the question of whether a person is really incorporated in the authentic community that celebrates the Sacrament.

Bourke and Meyendorff go on to interpret this understanding in terms of present relations between Orthodox and Roman Catholics. In these communions, to be in the church is to be in communion with the bishop. But from the Roman Catholic standpoint, the college of bishops has no authority "unless it is simultaneously conceived of in terms of its head, the Roman Pontiff," so that the authority of the Orthodox bishops is not recognized, and sharing in communion between Orthodox and Roman Catholics is not possible. The same applies to every case in which the Orthodox bishops are not recognized by other communions, whatever the logic of this nonrecognition may be.

The question obviously arises whether these relationships have to be considered only in terms of official interchurch relations, or whether it is possible for an individual Christian, or a group of Christians, to be in communion with the Orthodox Church. The language used by Bourke and Meyendorff seems to leave an opening at this point. They speak of the "total unity of the communicant with the bishop-celebrant of the Eucharist." But then they proceed to describe this unity as follows:

> Only if the communicant regards the bishop as possessing authority in worship, teaching, and governing, can he be said to be in union with him. This does not mean, of course, that the communicant need be under the authority of the particular bishop with whom he communicates, but he must at least recognize him as a bishop of the Church in the fullest sense.

The application of this principle would be for the bishop to decide in each particular case. Discussion of such matters among the Orthodox has traditionally come under the heading of what is called "economy." This word is an anglicization of the Greek *oikonomia,* which means "housekeeping," and, of course, has verbal links to the term "ecumenical." "Economy," then, is the housekeeping by which the Orthodox community orders its relations to other Christian churches.

There is much debate about what "economy" means,[33] some of the discussion seeming to seek to reduce it to one or another principle of canon law familiar in the West. Some say it is the equivalent of the Western idea of "dispensation." Others feel it can be understood in terms of the ideas of "validity" and "efficacy" of the Sacrament. But to read this debate is to realize that defining "economy" is like trying to turn a family saying into a logical principle. In these matters there will certainly be clarification and development, but it is likely to be along lines of family tradition, not along lines that outside observers might try to impose.

What is the family tradition? If anything, it is a kind of Eastern populism. The people have always been primary in Orthodoxy. It is *their* tradition that counts, not the detached views of a priestly caste. The transfer of Orthodox peoples to pluralistic Western environments, the spread of secularization and pluralism in their original homelands, all these things create conditions this people has not previously had to face. There will be changes. Their exact nature and timing are unpredictable, but the changes will come first in actual practice. Theological explanation, always loosely formulated, will follow the practice.

Meanwhile the Orthodox emphasis on the wholeness of the life of a universal worshiping community has much to offer Western minds. There are ways in which the new understandings of Christian peoplehood, dealt with in these pages, might be more easily recognized and assimilated within Orthodoxy than they are likely to be in their own church surroundings. Orthodox participation in ecumenical affairs will continue to be vigorous. Orthodoxy will continue to insist that active ecumenism is not inconsistent with communal integrity as a people: indeed they will continue to insist and to show that the two things go together.

2. THE ROMAN CATHOLIC CHURCH

The Roman Catholic situation is more complex because this church has had a greater variety of contacts with other forms of Christian community. The pattern of development remains the same, however. An understanding of the church emerging from the "centralist" (Swanson) church-society syntheses characteristic of medieval Western Europe needs little legislation regulating external relationships until it encounters confessional, religious, and cultural pluralism. It then gradually evolves into a free-standing ecclesiastical structure that persists, with certain

changes, long after the social circumstances that gave rise
to its root metaphor have vanished.

The story is too long and complex to be told in detail.[34]
Suffice it to say that the classical provisions of Roman
Catholic canon law, which, before Vatican II, made it
illicit for the faithful in any way actively to assist or to
take part in the worship of non-Catholic bodies, were
largely a result of two encounters with pluralism. The first
was with Eastern Orthodox Christians in the Middle East,
and the second was with Protestant groups in Northern
Europe.

Political circumstances in the Middle East both before
and after the Turkish conquest of Constantinople in 1453
threw ecclesiastically separated Roman Catholics and
Orthodox into a variety of contacts with each other. The
hope of winning some of the Orthodox groups back to
Rome led the popes before 1453 to be relatively open on
the question of shared worship. After the Turkish takeover,
Moslem customs and laws relating to the Christian community in these lands made such sharing necessary if
contact was to be retained and any hope of reunion kept
alive. It was not until the Counter-Reformation in the
West produced a hardening of attitudes and, in particular,
a greatly increased sensitivity to the issue of doctrinal
heresy that Rome began to issue decrees banning participation by Catholics in non-Catholic services. The very strict
enactment of 1729 stresses errors of faith to be found in
the Orthodox liturgies. By 1859 we are hearing the argument that Communion is a sign of churchly community,
and hence one ought not to celebrate it with those outside
the community. Clearly experience with Protestants had
affected Catholic attitudes toward the Orthodox as well,
and by the nineteenth century Rome felt beleaguered. This
was the eve of Vatican I. The cultural unity of Europe was
shattered and the effort to maintain a closed Christian
community by canon law reached its height. What began

as a natural, externally unchallenged unity of church and culture became a series of exclusive ecclesiastical claims over against both culture and other Christians.

Such was the situation in the Roman Catholic Church until the massive reconsideration that broke out into the open at Vatican II. The work of this most recent Council demands the lion's share of attention because it sets forth the principles and applications of Catholic churchmanship now in effect. In general, Vatican II takes steps toward the recognition of a wider catholicity. Without abandoning the claim that the Roman Church embodies the essential unity and wholeness of apostolic faith, the enactments of Vatican II modify the exclusiveness of earlier Catholic positions. Most of the relevant material can be found in a document of the Council, the *Decree on Ecumenism*.[35]

Both sides, it is said, were at fault in the original separations between East and West and between Protestants and Catholics. Later generations born into already separated communions cannot be blamed. The Catholic Church looks upon them as brothers because "men who believe in Christ and have been truly baptized are in real communion with the Catholic Church even though this communion is imperfect." Differences in doctrine, discipline, and structure indeed create many obstacles that the ecumenical movement is trying to overcome. Yet the "separated brethren" possess many of the "significant elements and endowments which together go to build up and give life to the Church" and, in addition, they celebrate "many liturgical actions of the Christian religion." Further, "these liturgical actions must be regarded as capable of giving access to that communion in which is salvation."

The deficiency of these separated churches and communities is subtly expressed. They "are not blessed with that unity which Jesus Christ wished to bestow on all those who through him were born again into one body." They can only "benefit fully from the means of salvation . . .

through Christ's Catholic Church." The first of these two propositions simply echoes what Protestants have constantly acknowledged themselves. The second presumably refers to the Roman Catholic Church but yet does not say so explicitly, leaving open the possibility of further interpretation in the direction of a broader understanding of catholicity.

Repeatedly the *Decree on Ecumenism* uses the expression "Communities and Churches" to refer to the ecclesial gatherings of separated brethren. This has given rise to the assumption that the *Decree* makes a distinction between non-Roman Catholic bodies, some deserving to be called "Churches" and some only "Communities." Perhaps this is so, but the *Decree* takes care never to say which non-Roman bodies are which. Thus we are in the presence of a distinction made but not applied. Elsewhere it is made clear that the non-Roman bodies are considered to vary so much among themselves that they can be placed in no single category and any dialogue or negotiation would have to be pursued with each non-Roman confessional grouping separately. The *Decree* seems to use the phrase *communicatio in sacris* to refer generally to common worship of every kind between Roman Catholics and the "separated brethren." The language here deserves quotation in full.

In certain special circumstances, such as the prescribed prayers "for unity," and during ecumenical gatherings, it is allowable, and indeed desirable, that Catholics should join in prayer with their separated brethren. Such prayers in common are certainly an effective means of obtaining the grace of unity, and they are a true expression of the ties which still bind Catholics to their separated brethren. "For where two or three are gathered together in my name, there am I in the midst of them" (Mt. 18:20).

Yet worship in common (*communicatio in sacris*) is not to be considered as a means to be used indiscriminately for the restoration of Christian unity. There are two main principles governing the practice of such common worship: first, the bearing witness to the unity of the Church, and second, the sharing in the means of grace. Witness to the unity of the Church very generally forbids common worship to Christians, but the grace to be had from it sometimes commends this practice. The course to be adopted, with due regard to all the circumstances of time, place, and persons, is to be decided by local episcopal authority, unless otherwise provided for by the Bishop's Conference according to its statutes, or by the Holy See.[36]

The *Decree* later applies these principles somewhat differently to the separated churches of the East and of the West. Of the Eastern churches the *Decree* says:

These Churches, although separated from us yet possess true sacraments, and above all, by apostolic succession, the priesthood and the Eucharist, whereby they are linked with us in closest intimacy. Therefore some worship in common (*communicatio in sacris*), given suitable circumstances and the approval of Church authority, is not merely possible but to be encouraged.[37]

Nothing comparable is said about common worship with the separated Western churches. It is said that

. . . they have not retained the authentic and full reality of the eucharistic mystery, especially because of the absence of the sacrament of Orders, nevertheless when they commemorate his death and resurrection in the Lord's Supper, they profess that it signifies life in communion with Christ and look forward to his coming in glory. . . . Moreover, their form of worship not seldom displays notable features of the liturgy which they shared with us of old.[38]

Dialogue concerning the meaning of worship should take place with the separated brethren of the West, but actual common worship with them is, presumably, to be guided by the general principles for *communicatio* already outlined.

Taken in itself, the *Decree on Ecumenism* leaves a remarkable amount of freedom to the bishop to decide what forms of common worship will and will not take place in his diocese.

No specific definition or limitation is placed on the "prayers in common," *preces communes,* which are said to be "an effective means of obtaining the grace of unity, and . . . a true expression of the ties which still bind Catholics to their separated brethren." Nor is it specifically said that *communicatio in sacris* can mean liturgical prayer only where Roman Catholic–Orthodox relations are concerned. Certainly a difference of attitude is implied in what is later said about the separated brethren of East and West, but hard and fast conclusions are (apparently deliberately) not drawn from this difference, nor does the difference find mention among the broad theological principles that are to guide bishops in making their decisions about specific cases.

The latter principles deserve attention in and of themselves. *Communicatio in sacris* cannot be thought to bear witness to the unity of the church because that unity is not yet visibly realized. On the other hand, it may make possible a sharing in the means of grace, and the grace thus to be had "sometimes commends this practice." It should be noted, furthermore, that the words of the *Decree* do not refer to the question of Orders, or of beliefs about the Eucharist, or even of doctrinal agreement in general, as contraindications to *communicatio in sacris.* Not that it denies the relevance of these things, but the *Decree* places the whole matter on the broader ground of witness to the unity of Christ's church, and of the grace that even separated Christians can share.

It is important to see that these principles, in and of themselves, do not rule out any particular form of common worship up to and including common participation in the Eucharist. Interpretations of the *Decree* (see below) tend to argue that since the Eucharist is a celebration of accomplished unity, this is ruled out. But the *Decree,* carefully, does not say so. On the contrary, this document leaves the interpreter to judge when, and under what conditions, an act of common worship should be regarded as bearing witness to a nonexistent unity and when it should be regarded as a form of prayer for the grace of unity. The distinction drawn is not between the Eucharist and other forms of worship but between appropriate and inappropriate circumstances. Further, a theologian might well ask whether there does not lie behind this formulation the issue whether unity *is* a human accomplishment or a gift of grace. The future interpretation of the *Decree* may well depend on the development of eucharistic theology among Roman Catholic and other theologians. The point to be made now, of course, is that the *Decree on Ecumenism* is fully open-ended as regards the application of its principles. The option left to the bishops, and to the other authorities mentioned, is very broad indeed.

It must be said that *present* official interpretations of the *Decree* decidedly limit this range of options. This is understandable. But no directory for the application of the decisions of Vatican II has the same authority as the Council's enactments themselves. Without in any way questioning the propriety of a limited application of the *Decree* by church authorities at the outset, most observers agree that much scope for further ecumenical development is already present in the texts of Vatican II, and that this development is bound to take place.

The *Directory for the Application of the Decisions of the Second Ecumenical Council of the Vatican Concerning Ecumenical Matters,* dated May 14, 1967, is the present standard. More than half this document is concerned with matters of policy within the Roman Catholic Church itself: the setting up of diocesan ecumenical commissions, dealing with the question of the baptism of converts from other Christian bodies, the fostering of "spiritual ecumenism,"

including prayer for unity, among Roman Catholics themselves. The importance of these intramural items for the
process of ecumenical growth should not be overlooked.
We are interested, however, in the position of the *Directory*
as regards common worship. The root of the position here
lies in a distinction that *may* be implied by the *Decree on
Ecumenism* but which is not expressed there in so many
words: a distinction between *communicatio in sacris* and
preces communes. The former term now means participation in the official liturgical worship of another church or
ecclesial community. The latter means participation in
prayer services which have no such official status in the life
of any organized Christian body but which may be organized on ecumenical or national occasions of various sorts.

Preces communes create no difficulty. If anything, this
form of common worship, at the appropriate times and
places, is encouraged. It is the sharing of liturgical worship, or *communicatio in sacris,* that raises difficulties. As
regards the Eastern churches, there is no problem from the
Roman Catholic side. The *Directory* confines itself to practical admonitions designed to promote orderly procedure
and to avoid scandal or misunderstanding. The major
difficulty here is raised by the principle of reciprocity,
which, while it is not defined in the document, suggests
that the actual sharing in liturgical worship between
Roman Catholics and Orthodox would require both sides to
extend the same privileges to each other. At the present
time there is doubt about this from the Orthodox side.

As regards all other separated brethren, the *Directory* is
very reserved, although not without an element of apparent
and probably deliberate ambiguity.

Since the sacraments are both signs of unity and sources
of grace the Church can for adequate reasons allow access to
those sacraments to a separated brother. This may be permitted in danger of death or in urgent need (during persecu-
tion, in prisons) if the separated brother has no access to a

minister of his own communion, and spontaneously asks a Catholic priest for the sacraments—so long as he declares a faith in these sacraments in harmony with that of the Church, and is rightly disposed. . . . A Catholic in similar circumstances may not ask for these sacraments except from a minister who has been validly ordained.[39]

The question here, as Roman Catholic observers (e.g., Father Gregory Baum)[40] have pointed out, is that of the meaning of "adequate reasons." The examples given are all instances of urgent necessity, i.e., extreme circumstances that go beyond what one might assume "adequate reasons" to mean. Do adequate reasons not include friendship, ecumenical concern, mixed marriage, or growth in holiness? It would seem, as Fr. Baum points out, that if adequate reasons are limited to the cases of extreme need, the practice of the Roman Catholic Church in this area has not changed as a result of Vatican II at all. Clearly the *Decree on Ecumenism* gives much scope for further development in thought and practice at this point.

Significant, too, is the requirement that a separated brother declare a faith in the sacraments "in harmony with that of the Church." We are not told exactly what this means: whether, indeed, it goes beyond the rudimentary doctrine of "intention" as it applies to Roman Catholic believers in general, that they intend what the church intends without further specification of detail. For here the possibility might be open to develop a doctrine of catholic intention in the wider ecumenical sense in which members of many different communions could share.

In passing, we may also note that when a Roman Catholic who in similar circumstances wishes to receive the Sacrament from a non-Roman Catholic minister, the validity of that minister's ordination is the deciding factor. But nothing is said about the practical application of the principle. Presumably the orders of the Eastern churches are in view here. What other ministerial orders are considered valid? Is this confined to Old Catholics, or is there a reference here to the Anglican Communion?

Finally, the *Directory* deals with the question of attendance, short of receiving the Sacrament, by Roman Catholics at non-Roman services, and vice versa. There seems to be no obstacle, if such attendance is only occasional, to a sharing, in either case, of the responses, hymns, and actions of the community whose liturgy is being celebrated if such participation does not include actually receiving the sacramental elements. The possibilities inherent in this may be greater than the writers of the *Directory* had in mind. For from some theological standpoints the language and action of the liturgy already in some sense mediate the presence of Christ. And, presumably, in doing so they are not necessarily "at variance with Catholic faith." An intriguing possibility in the present structure of the Mass will furnish an example. The "prayer of the faithful" marks the point at which those present are invited to add their particular intentions to those of the universal church. Might not a Protestant, under this rubric, add his own intentions to those being offered in the course of the Mass, and might not those intentions be eucharistic in character? The principal obstacle to such an understanding would be that mentioned by Gregory Baum in the article already cited: "the faithful," in the present language of the Mass, means simply Roman Catholics. The permission in the *Directory* for non-Roman Catholics to participate in the liturgy, however, already changes this situation in principle. And the same is reciprocally true of the situation that arises when Roman Catholics attend and participate in the eucharistic liturgy of another Christian body. Whether they literally receive the Sacrament or not, surely *their* intention becomes part of the celebration, and ecumenical progress is made.

As for the actual application of the principles of the *Directory,* this, as we have seen, for the most part is in the hands of the bishops, who must judge each situation as it arises. The nature of the case prevents research into the character of such episcopal decisions as they are actually being made, or into the chains of reasoning actually being followed. It can be said that numerous exceptions are already being made, particularly in the case of nuptial masses in connection with mixed marriages, but also in other forms of *communicatio in sacris* as well.

3. THE ANGLICAN COMMUNION

The thesis that modern church positions tend to be theologically and institutionally rationalized extensions of models of church life connected with vanished sociocultural worlds receives further confirmation in the history of Anglicanism.[41] From the beginning, Anglicans have held two assumptions clearly colored by the circumstances of the sixteenth century in which important features of Anglican polity emerged. Ecclesiastically, they have seen themselves as continuous with the ancient Catholic Church of their land: independent of Rome and reformed from within to be sure, but clearly the *historic* English church. Politically they have also understood themselves to be the *national* church, headed on earth by the sovereign of the realm. In their original setting, these assumptions seemed wholly natural and they generated little canonical legislation to cover relations with other Christians. It was only with the Act of Uniformity in 1662, and through a complex history afterward, that Anglicanism began to become a distinct "communion."

It is impossible to say exactly, for example, when Anglicans and Roman Catholics really became distinguishable groups.[42] The Act of Supremacy of 1534 released English churchmen, so far as civil law was concerned, from the authority of the Pope, and, technically, this implied some sort of schism between those who acknowledged Henry VIII's hegemony and those who maintained loyalty to Rome. But the distinction became a difference only gradually. "Roman" Catholics continued to frequent the parish churches (although they reportedly preferred not to be seen entering or leaving with "Anglicans"), much of the old ritual was retained, the doctrine of the real presence continued to be maintained. Sometimes old rite and new rite were celebrated side by side. It was only the Council of Trent in its third and last period (1562–1563) that put a stop to these practices. By 1570, of course, Pius V's bull *Regnans in Excelsis* excommunicated Queen Elizabeth and set the seal on Anglican–Roman Catholic division.

As for relations with other "protestants," Anglicans were revising their liturgy and doctrine along lines they knew to be parallel to certain thrusts taking place in the Continental Reformation, all the while retaining the essential forms they had inherited from the pre-Reformation church. Before 1662, and in some ways afterward, the question of relationships with the Continental Protestants and with like-minded "dissenters" in England remained fluid. Many Anglicans in the sixteenth and seventeenth centuries saw no difficulty in receiving Communion from Protestant ministers in Holland and France, and some were equally open to the ministrations of dissenters at home. Even those who staunchly defended the importance of episcopal ordination in England generally refused to unchurch Protestant bodies abroad for their lack of it. And five or six ministers from the Continent, none of them with episcopal ordination, were given parishes in the Church of England before the Act of Uniformity forbade it.

It is clear that the issue here was that of building an indigenous English Christian community, not that of setting standards for others to meet. Yet the continued existence of other bodies of Christians in the same land eventually proved an embarrassment to the church order, "catholic" and national, according to which this indigenous community was being built. By 1662 the rupture with Rome was complete, and it had become clear that dissenters—Congregationalists, Presbyterians, Baptists, Quakers—were not going to join the Church of England on its terms. The Act of Uniformity of that year was designed to make the status of Anglicanism as the national church both legal and definitive. In doing this, the Act set in motion the process by which Anglicanism evolved as a distinct communion with canonical obstacles between itself and other Christian bodies.

The Act of Uniformity is striking evidence of the relation between this communion and the political and cultural conditions of seventeenth-century England. The Book of Common Prayer, still the liturgical standard in the Church of England and, with modifications, that of other Anglican bodies, is actually a part of the full text of this act of Parliament. It is both the church's service book *and* an artifact of the society in which the church lived. And the regulation regarding the admission of persons to Communion is part of this prayer book. It reads, innocently enough, as follows:

And there shall none be admitted to the Holy Communion, until such time as he be confirmed, or be ready and desirous to be confirmed.

The confirmation mentioned, of course, is confirmation by a bishop. That is to say, admission to Communion involves one's inclusion within a system of church order that itself strongly resembles the kind of "limited centralist" (Swanson) order characteristic of England. Subsidiary political units, then as now, represented the sovereign, but they possessed more freedom to give effect to this sovereignty in their own way than was characteristic of centralist regimes. So in Anglicanism—a central administration, a degree of hierarchy, but a wide range of theological and administrative options so long as the unity of the church is maintained *liturgically,* so long as *Communion* remains unbroken.

These tendencies, combined with Anglicanism's status as the English national church, produced in the seventeenth century an unsurprising series of anomalies. In *some* sense dissenters were still included in its membership, and for this very reason Anglicans could not recognize dissenting bodies as separate and independent churches. Some dissenters themselves indicated their recognition of this situation by the practice of occasional "conformity," that is, receiving Communion in the Anglican parish church from time to time as a gesture. This practice was understood and accepted by many on the Anglican side, although, for the most part, Anglicans were unable to reciprocate, fearing to give dissent a status they hesitated to confer. Similar practices were followed, for the same reasons, after the Methodist secession in the eighteenth century.

Yet for all its status as a national church, Anglicanism was also becoming a denomination, one Christian body in an increasingly pluralistic situation. It was in denominational form, obviously, that Anglicanism was exported overseas. Outside England Anglican churches do not claim to have spiritual oversight of whole populations, nor do members of other churches expect Anglican priests to supply their sacramental needs.

It is not surprising that in England today the original intention of the confirmation rubric and its present legal status are subjects of renewed debate. The declaration in the prayer book preface "Of Ceremonies" says:

In these our doings we condemn no other nations, nor prescribe anything but to our own people only.

The legal question is whether "our own people" means Anglicans or Englishmen. Archbishop Tait's judgment of

1870 clearly assumes that "our own people" means Anglicans, since he excepts "members of foreign or dissenting bodies who occasionally conform."[43] There have been many Anglicans, however, who have thought otherwise, and indeed an opinion of the Legal Board of the Church Assembly in 1967 stated the view that the Act, Book, and rubrics "were intended to bind all subjects of the realm and not members of the Church of England alone."[44] Study of the precedents and arguments involved suggests that so far as the civil law is concerned, the Legal Board may well be right. But then the actual practice of many parishes of the Church of England has been at variance with the law for more than three hundred years.

It is evident, in any case, that the Confirmation rubric functions differently outside England. The same words appear in the prayer books used in other Anglican provinces, for example, that of the Protestant Episcopal Church in the U.S.A. Here beyond the jurisdiction of the Act of Uniformity, the rubric is no longer tied to the sociocultural situation that produced it, but is, rather, a survival of that situation which must be given new meanings as the situation demands.

In England, the eighteenth and nineteenth centuries saw increasing polarization over the question of Anglicanism's true character. On the one hand, the foreign missionary movement and the growth of evangelical or broad churchmanship favored a policy of openness toward members and ministers of other Christian groups. German and Danish Lutheran ministers were employed by Anglican missionary societies in India for a century, a fact that suggests the real issue was the integrity of churchly community in England itself, not the status of other ministries as such. Furthermore, evangelical Anglicans began to invite dissenters to Communion at church conferences, and this practice spread to certain parishes. In some cases these invitations were reciprocated, and some Anglicans received

Communion from dissenting clergy.

On the other hand, the first half of the nineteenth century saw the growth of the Oxford Movement, which fostered a reawakened sense of Anglicanism's continuity with the early and medieval church, and with it a greater emphasis on the importance of catholic order. In some respects a response to the apparent danger of secularism and to the loss of ecclesiastical privileges, the movement placed emphasis on the divine nature and commission of the church. All of this was associated with a doctrine of apostolic succession that placed an episcopal church in a position different from that of other Christian groups. Adherents of these tendencies became far more wary of nonconformity, and came to regard the admission of non-Anglicans to Communion as a violation of church order.

These two viewpoints, with variations, are visible in contemporary Anglicanism. Yet there has been a resistance to further binding legislation on the issue of Communion. So pluralistic and mobile has the situation become that the Lambeth Conferences and provincial resolutions have tended to stress general principles, leaving application of them to the bishop having jurisdiction in any given case. The Lambeth Conference of 1930 followed this line, citing as a "general rule" that "members of Anglican Churches should receive Holy Communion only from ministers of their own Church," but acknowledging that there might be circumstances where this was impossible. The Conference had in mind mainly situations outside England, but its wording could have been more broadly applied. By 1933, the provinces of Canterbury and York were ready to suggest guidelines for receiving non-Anglicans at Anglican services. Three points were made: non-Anglicans cut off from their own churches were welcome, at least temporarily; non-Anglicans in school or college communities with Anglican chapels could take Communion while in residence; other Christians meeting with

Anglicans for ecumenical purposes could receive the Sacrament at the Anglican rite—all this, of course, with the bishop approving.

These provisions, together with others like them in the different provinces, constituted the basic Anglican stance until 1968. The 1958 Lambeth Conference declined to recommend the further step of "reciprocal intercommunion" with Presbyterians, then engaged in union discussions in England and Scotland. The 1967 American Episcopal General Convention, on the other hand, authorized a liberal interpretation of the basic Anglican stance by welcoming outsiders on the basis of "individual spiritual need," without specifying just what circumstances this might include. Bishops generally became more liberal, and in some dioceses the policy moved toward the position of open Communion. But nothing more definitive was said until the publication, in 1968, of a report entitled *Intercommunion Today*. This statement, its general terms endorsed by the 1968 Lambeth Conference, contains a proposal that, if adopted by the different provinces, would materially change the Anglican situation.

Acknowledging that there continues to be strong support among Anglicans for the traditional "Catholic" and "Protestant" viewpoints, *Intercommunion Today* outlines a third position. Ecumenical progress, not to speak of the state of the modern world, places Christians in an unprecedented situation. Conclusions that were valid in past generations may not be so now. In such a context it may be right for Christians to share in common sacramental actions that seemed impossible a few years ago. Contextual factors *may* recommend that Communion between separated Christians take place. The report says:

The tension must always be held between the fact that to receive communion in disunity is merely to deepen our sin and the fact that it is the one loaf which alone has power to

create unity out of our disunity. Only deep spiritual "discern-
ment," "examining" and "judging ourselves truly" (I Cor. 11:
27–32), can enable us to know the point at which mercy
rejoices over judgment and receiving communion together
becomes less sinful than receiving apart.[45]

This statement is theologically compatible with the position
of the *Decree on Ecumenism* of Vatican II, for, in different
language, it makes the same distinction between Communion as a sign of existing unity and Communion as a
source of grace in the search for unity. What will deter-
mine the actual practice to be followed will be pastoral,
that is, contextual, judgment.

For the moment, *Intercommunion Today* judges that
reciprocal intercommunion ought to be possible between
churches that have entered a solemn compact to move
toward union, even if all the theological and practical
problems are not solved. The report even queries whether
a formal statement by the churches in question is needed.
There may be other evidence that they have set out on the
path toward reconciliation. And once this underlying principle is accepted, still further possibilities come into view.
What about a decision based on the growing together of
small groups of Christians in a particular locality? What
ought to be the significance of the joint declaration of the
Pope and the Archbishop of Canterbury in March, 1966?

Anglicanism has thus long since moved toward a trans-
English catholicity. It reaches out toward Christians for
whom 1662 means nothing. But it remains true that
Anglican liturgical forms and church government bear the
marks of their origin. Whether the forms themselves make
it difficult to relate to new expressions of Christian community remains to be decided. With every other church,
Anglicanism faces a move not only from the homeland to
a wider Christian world, but from Christendom to a situation as yet undefined and unknown.

4. THE LUTHERAN CHURCHES

If Anglicanism is the extension of a community metaphor that secures continuity and legitimacy through the
"historic episcopate," the Lutheran churches perpetuate a
model that seeks to accomplish the same ends by means of
verbal confessions of faith. The political situation out of
which Lutheranism emerged is similar, in Swanson's typology, to that which formed the background of the Anglican
development. In both cases we find the church called to
legitimate a "limited centralist" regime, one in which the
unity of the body politic is conceived as issuing from a
single central authority, despite the fact that local units
enjoy a range of options in translating this sovereignty into
practical terms.

Thus one must understand not only Luther's personal
discovery of the gospel of justification by faith but also the
political context in which he and his successors made this
discovery the basis of a new form of Christian gathering.
The Lutheran Reformation took place within the context
of the Holy Roman Empire: a loose imperium combining
political units of many kinds as a mainly symbolic, but
occasionally potent, continuation of the supposed unity of
medieval Europe. The Roman Catholic Church furnished
the religious legitimation for this vast and varied political
ordering. The unity of Christendom, conceived in these or
similar terms, meant much to Luther. Moreover, the
princedoms and duchies in which the decisions to opt for
Lutheranism or Roman Catholicism were eventually made
themselves reflected the same sort of political order. Conversion to Lutheranism was only in limited degree a decision for the individual. Lutheranism became a social reality
by the decision of whole political units. *Cuius regio, eius
religio* was the principle: "whoever the ruler is, his religion
prevails in his realm," to translate and interpret this saying.
Luther's antipathy for what he saw as distortions of the

gospel at the hands of Rome was matched by his concern for the religious unity and freedom of "the German nation," or "the Christian nobility of the German nation" to whom he addressed so many appeals. Thus the Lutheran understanding of the church begins as a political indigenization of the consequences of Luther's understanding of justification. It is not a series of inferences drawn from this doctrine in the abstract.

That continuity and legitimacy in this understanding of the church is expressed in confessional documents is perhaps a consequence of the particular nature of Luther's discovery of justification as he expounded the Bible, with his conviction that every man could do the same. The resulting confessions of faith had somewhat the same *function* as bishops in the community. The Augsburg Confession of 1530 is notable for its stress on the right (*recte*) preaching of the gospel and the right administration of the Sacraments. This "rightness" was a matter of fidelity both to a proper understanding of the New Testament and to the community norm. The Confession was more than an intellectual exercise: it represented the presence and power of Christ in formulating what "right" preaching and celebration meant. Luther's insistence in his debate with Ulrich Zwingli, at Marburg in 1529, upon the real presence of Christ "in, with, and under" the bread, the wine, and the Word was another expression of the same conviction. Thus the Lutheran preacher was free to use his ingenuity in expounding the gospel so long as his fidelity to the confessional standard ensured that the power of Christ is properly represented in his preaching and in his conduct of the liturgy, and hence really present. The Roman Catholic understanding of the Sacrament, which Luther rejected, appeared to involve an understanding of immanence that left no room for God's free grace or for man's response to it in faith.

The affinity of this understanding of unity and freedom in the Christian community as such with the political requirements of unity and freedom in the Christendom of Luther's time is striking. Subsequent Lutheran developments have projected this position upon new contexts: sometimes appropriately to the cultural and political situation as in Scandinavia, sometimes in such a way as to create cultural and ethnic ghettos as in North America. The pressure to maintain unity through the confessional definition of right preaching and right celebration has, in fact, led to divisions between Lutherans themselves. Does rightness mean adherence to the whole range of doctrinal assertions contained in the Lutheran Confessions, or does it mean substantial agreement on essential doctrines only? And if the latter, who is to decide what doctrines are essential? Furthermore, is the standard of rightness to be applied to the official confessional positions of churches only, or is it to be applied to the views of individuals too?

These questions have become acute as isolation between Lutheran and other Christian groups has been broken down, as new generations have emerged for whom the old cultural syntheses mean less and less. In America, Lutheranism has come some distance from the "Akron Decision" (1870) and the "Galesburg Rule" (1875), which affirmed, in virtually identical words, "Lutheran pulpits for Lutheran ministers only, Lutheran altars for Lutheran communicants only."[46] Today, as the American Lutheran Church says in its *Statement on Church Fellowship* (1964), "it is recognized that, in the application of these principles, situations calling for exceptions will arise. The individual Christian, the conscientious pastor, the local congregation, and the church bodies, in determining their attitudes in such situations, must earnestly seek the guidance of the Holy Spirit and the instruction of the inspired Word." The Lutheran Church in America has adopted a statement entitled *Communion Practices* (1964), which warns that "no practice should be encouraged which uses the Lord's Supper to imply a unity which is not a reality in other realms of faith and order," and urges that "services shall set forth without reservation the church's doctrine of the Lord's Supper." But the same document permits Lutheran pastors to officiate on ecumenical occasions provided certain safeguards are maintained, and, as for individual Lutherans in other Christian churches, "the individual must decide for himself when and where such participation is in order. He should not disregard the church's doctrine concerning the Sacrament. Yet he should know that Christ's presence does not depend on the liturgical orders used or the ministers in charge."

Modern statements by Lutheran theologians stress that the existence of genuine community in Christ is the decisive criterion for sacramental sharing. Agreement on doctrine is a mark of community, not a standard to be applied in the abstract. Here Lutherans are in total agreement with Orthodox, Roman Catholics, Anglicans, and many others. The only question is that of how and where real Christian community is to be found. It follows from this position that the admission of individual Christians of other communions to the Sacrament raises few problems, provided these individuals understand what they are doing. The real problems are connected with communion fellowship between Lutherans and other organized Christian bodies. In the latter case the classical issues still arise. What do the "right" preaching and the "right" celebration mean outside the context established by the Lutheran confessions? Luther and his followers were trying to restore the integrity and the unity of Christendom, as they knew it, on the basis of these confessions. But the Christendom they knew was that of the Holy Roman Empire, with its particular political institutions and assumptions about the structure of human community. And the Holy Roman Empire has vanished.

Conversations have been under way for some years between Lutheran and other Christian theologians to clarify what a wider understanding of Christian community should mean. Concrete results have been achieved particularly in Lutheran-Reformed dialogue. The Arnoldshain Theses (1953) are a Lutheran-Reformed agreement on the meaning of Holy Communion, and sacramental sharing now exists in Germany, France, and the Netherlands on the basis of this theological achievement. In principle, there is no reason why similar agreements should not in time be worked out between Lutherans and other Christian bodies.

5. THE REFORMED CHURCHES

The Reformed family of churches is one of the most diverse Christian groupings. It includes most churches descended in various ways from the work of John Calvin: those which have the name "Reformed" as well as those known as "Presbyterian," and including such "pre-Reformation" bodies as the Waldensian Church, the Church of the Czech Brethren. The Reformed tradition also flows strongly in certain united communities, such as, in America, the United Church of Christ. Reformed influence, in the form of variant versions of Calvinism, has also been significant in the life of the various "free churches," especially in England.

Despite the diversity of historical experience that the Reformed churches have known, they feed on certain common community metaphors that have influenced both their theology and their polity. Most of the Reformed churches had their origin in political communities organized differently from those which gave birth to Lutheranism. Largely outside the Holy Roman Empire, and very often in permanent minority status, the Reformed churches emerged in interaction with the appearance of a new conception of the body politic. No longer a fabric in which harmony with the will of central authority gave the magistrate his "right," this conception saw society as an arena in which diverse organized groups with different and often conflicting interests might coordinate their claims according to a constitutional process. This meant that no political instrument could be thought to carry or represent divine authority. On the contrary, the available political analogies suggested that God, though active in his creation, was not to be identified with any power within it.

It is striking that the societies in which Calvinism took root generally corresponded to this political pattern. "Balanced regimes" in Swanson's typology (Geneva, Bohemia, Hungary, Transylvania, the Scottish lowlands, Cleves, Mark) in which the ruler's power was countered by councils representing organized nongovernmental groups, and "heterarchic regimes" (four Swiss cantons and the Netherlands) with no single ruler at all but only constant interaction between representatives of different constituent bodies, account for most Reformed origins. And Reformed churchmanship quickly spread to groups having an interest in such democratization but living under other kinds of regimes: French Protestants and English Puritans for example.

The interaction between visions of community and theological metaphors in these different situations does much to explain the forms that Reformed Christianity took. No more than in the other cases we have examined does this mean that the church was religious legitimator of culture and nothing else. It means rather that the Biblical message demanded theological articulation and social form, and that these had to be "relevant" to their setting. In the Reformed case, the most notable trait was the belief in the transcendence of God, the refusal to identify any of man's works with God's power or presence. This carried with it the conviction that being part of a Christian culture did not automatically mean that one was included in God's Kingdom. Moreover, there was nothing one could do, in culture

or in church, to guarantee, or even enhance, one's chances
for election. There might be *evidence* that one was of the
elect, but this was fully in God's hands, not in the hands of
men. The elect, for Calvin, were never an identifiable
social group. This was the very opposite of the immanental
doctrine of sovereignty and the social order.

The forms of Christian community that grew out of
these convictions tended to a stress on orderly representative procedures within and to considerable openness to
other Christian groups without. And what was true of
church government was also true of theological statements and their function. At first reluctant to compose
confessional statements at all (Calvin's own church in
Geneva did not make "Calvinism" its official position) for
fear that this would obscure the continuity of the Reformed churches with the ancient and medieval church,
the gradual hardening of ecclesiastical lines after the Reformation led to a progressive rationalizing of the Reformed position. There was a tendency to assume that even
if God's decrees are inscrutable, the logic by which he
proceeds must be as orderly as a presbytery agenda. From
the sixteenth-century evangelical piety of the Scots Confession and the Heidelberg Catechism, confessional development moved to the rationalism of seventeenth-century
documents, such as the Westminster Confession. Here
confidence that man can understand the *logic* of salvation
combined with certainty that he can never know how God
will apply this logic to any individual case, reaches its
height.

The tendency to impose tight theological discipline
within the church, as for example in Puritan New England, seems to have been the result both of the sense of
precariousness in man's hold on salvation and of the precariousness of the new political communities that Reformed churchmen were forming. Yet the firm ideological
control existing within the Reformed churches was not

extended to relations between Reformed and other Christian groups. The Reformed churches would characteristically expect other bodies to be as theologically serious as they themselves, but would not expect them to adhere to the same confessional statements. This attitude again seems to reflect on a larger scale the idea of a body politic constituted by the tension between different organized interests, not by an organic structure every part of which expressed quasi-divine royal power.

Consistent with this is the fact that Reformed churches have generally been open to receiving Communion in other churches, to welcoming other Christians to their own Sacraments, and to participation in cooperative and united Christian enterprises of various kinds. They have seen little need for elaborate legislation on such questions. The 1954 statement of the World Alliance of Reformed Churches, reaffirmed in 1964, strikingly reflects what has been implicit in Reformed history. No human institution carries divine authority: "The Table of the Lord is His, not ours. We believe that we dare not refuse the sacrament to any baptized person who loves and confesses Jesus Christ as Lord and Savior." And why not work these matters out between the churches in an orderly and candid way? "We would welcome face to face talks with our fellow Christians in other Churches looking towards the time when all sincere Christians will be welcome around a common table."[47]

Thus there are few obstacles from the Reformed side to any form of sacramental sharing. For many Reformed Christians today this includes openness to Roman Catholics and to Orthodox as well as to other Protestants. Such obstacles as existed to acceptance of Roman Catholic sacraments in the past were not legislated restraints, but rather a combination of doubt about the theological implications of the Mass with attitudes understandably derived from unfortunate encounters with the Roman Church. Polemics against Rome are found with some frequency in certain of the sixteenth- and seventeenth-century Reformed confessions. This viewpoint has changed in the light of new understandings on both sides concerning the nature of worship and on the basis of contacts that breed mutual confidence and understanding. As for the Orthodox, most Reformed churches are only beginning to see ecumenical possibilities. For the most part, Reformed and Orthodox Christians have been isolated from each other until modern times, despite some friction that still continues in connection with missionary efforts in the Middle East.

Yet it would be a mistake to equate this absence of Reformed restrictions on sacramental sharing with an ideal ecumenical stance. The marks of the political and social origins of Reformed polity still remain. They tend to produce attitudes that are one-sidedly practical, verbal, and, yes, bourgeois. Reformed theologians tend to be tolerant of the more immanental Christian traditions as well as the more enthusiastic, but they seldom understand profoundly these expressions of faith. The issue, therefore, arises for churches holding this general position of the responsible use of ecumenical freedom. With openness as regards participation in the Sacrament there often goes what looks to others like ignorance or indifference. This is not always an encouraging appearance with which to confront Christians who may be making spiritual sacrifices or risking ecclesiastical discipline in the ecumenical cause. The Reformed churches, just because of their openness, have more than the usual responsibility to reflect what it means for them to be offering their own Sacraments for ecumenical purposes. Can the Reformed tradition of open Communion, in short, bear this much freight?

6. The "Free Churches"

The term "free churches" is used here to refer to the

variety of Christian groups that originated not as religious expressions of the outlook of whole societies but as movements of dissent. This is to adopt an appellation common in England, where the "free churches" include virtually all Christian bodies that are not Anglican or Roman Catholic: e.g., Baptists, Methodists, Congregationalists, Quakers, Presbyterians, and so on. The point here is "dissenting" or minority status, not theological position or polity, which may be quite varied. The expression "free churches" can thus also be used for bodies of minority origin elsewhere: Baptists from the European continent, Mennonites, Moravians, and so on, and even for dissenting offshoots from the mainline American denominations. It seems the best general term for this kind of churchmanship, and one that also raises the question of how such groups are related to the rather different, experimental, "free" churches of today.

The present status of these denominations, let it be stressed, is not the issue, but rather the circumstances of their origins. Some have since become majority churches, or at least have acquired majority outlooks, as, for example, Baptists and Methodists in the American South. The emphasis on origin is a further attempt to test the hypothesis that root metaphors of the nature of sovereignity and community persist in Christian churches long after the social conditions of their beginnings have disappeared. In the case of dissenting bodies, however, we no longer have Swanson's theory to help us, for Swanson is concerned exclusively with Christian forms that were legally adopted by whole societies when they reached political settlements after the Reformation. In some instances, the "free churches" were those on the losing sides of these struggles. In other cases they were bodies, like the Methodists, resulting from later dissenting movements.

We are justified in taking these churches together not only because their separate histories are too long and diverse to recount but also because they represent a particular kind of church-society interaction. How, in short, does minority status affect the basic communal metaphor, and do distinctive traits of it show up in subsequent development? Is it important that these groups, despite their dissent, all somehow assume that society at large is "Christian," that is, that they dissent within a "Constantinian" framework? How does this distinguish them from dissenting groups today?

The "free churches" seem to have been strongly influenced by Calvinism. Repeatedly, this is the theological background one finds, even where it is considerably modified. Several reasons for this may be suggested. The "heterarchic" and "limited centralist" societies in which Calvinism flourished were far more hospitable to dissent than "centralist" or "commensal" orders. Such situations were more open to the attempt to construct one form or another of the holy commonwealth based, it was thought, directly on Biblical models. But beyond this, Calvinism itself contained a theological possibility that minority groups developed. Here lay the root of the idea that one could distinguish a community of the elect on the basis of evangelical experience.

Calvinism in its sixteenth-century Genevan form, it will be remembered, insists that the body of the elect does not appear in the form of any recognizable social grouping. Just as men cannot fathom God's decrees, so they cannot point out the distinctive social consequences of his electing will. A whole society can be built on the premise that the general nature of God's will is understood. But this society is a mixture of the elect and the nonelect and the society does not presume to tell the two apart. But is it not possible that when a Calvinistic community finds itself in minority status there are pressures to argue that the elect have now stepped forward in the form of the minority group?

Admittedly minority Calvinist churches hesitated to say

this in so many words. But with the need to justify the minority community's existence and to set up standards of membership, resort was had to various forms of the notion of evangelical experience, and it was difficult to maintain that such experience was not evidence of electing grace. Thus we may suggest that the community metaphors of Calvinist minorities represented the original Calvinist church-society pattern but did so in revisionist ways. The notion of a democratic "heterarchic" society was miniaturized to form the polity of the gathered group, and the doctrine of election was gradually projected in utopian terms to identify the group with the previously invisible elect company. The root metaphor of community and sovereignty still contained the same elements, but minority status had changed them around.

It is interesting to observe what Calvinists with experience in minority situations did when they subsequently found themselves in the majority position as social legitimators. They tended in the direction of elitist interpretations of election! Thus in Puritan New England, the notion that a certain kind of evangelical experience was putative evidence of election quickly produced a new kind of minority caste, this one on top of the social heap. In New England the evangelical experience had to be carefully defined and controlled, for persons outside the establishment could claim to have had it in competitive forms which, if they gained a following, could sunder the precariously existing commonwealth. The insecurities of the old minority psychology, combined with the very real economic and physical threats to the survival of the Puritan colonies, tended to exaggerate the elitist interpretation of election beyond what good Calvinist theologians were likely to accept, unless the sheer necessities of the situation forced them in this direction.

The forms of Calvinism adopted by Baptists, Methodists, and others moved ever farther from the rigidities of the Genevan and later Reformed scholastic models and closer to full reliance on the experiential standard partially embraced by Puritanism. Baptists, untempted by the Cromwellian possibility of actually capturing control of English society, developed a full-blown doctrine of local congregational autonomy—this together with the well-known insistence that membership in the congregation should be restricted to those who could profess the evangelical faith and be baptized as adults. Methodists, dissenting two centuries later within and then outside the Church of England, not only stressed the importance of warm evangelical experience but added a doctrine of perfecting grace to the Calvinist pattern. The latter led to an emphasis on the church as a moral community within the wider society, at times identifying election with the maintenance of certain standards of conduct.

The historical inadequacy of this sketch is obvious, but its purpose has been only to suggest an extension of the original hypothesis. That one can discern ecclesiastico-political root metaphors as clearly in dissenting forms of churchmanship as in others seems likely enough to warrant further study. The metaphors undergo a miniaturizing and utopianizing process that puts a premium on the believer's personal experience, but the archetypal social images, drawn from the experience of society at large, are unquestionably there.

The unanswerable question is whether the "free church" position, in any of its forms, is inherently better prepared for post-"Constantinian" conditions than majority forms of churchmanship. This will remain to be seen, but one suspects that the answer is "no." The essence of the "free church" position in its inception was a separatist witness to Biblical faith over against the rest of Christendom, at a time when Christianity represented the majority position of the culture. For the "free churches" to maintain the same stance within a "Christendom" *itself* now reduced to minority position, however, would not be to bear the same witness at all, but simply to be a sect within a sect. To maintain the same witness now would require the "free churches" to take a much more socially responsible position: to fight the battle for Biblical faith not in terms of polemics against majority Christianity but in terms of critical interaction with a non-Christian world. This, it would seem, "free" churches today are no better prepared to do than any others. By the time the "free churches" began to take on social responsibility, for the most part in the nineteenth century and afterward, they had already become denominations on the same footing as many Christian bodies that had begun life in the establishment. In some cases the only real indication of "free church" origins in these denominations became the class origins of their membership—hardly a special qualification for solving the modern church-world conundrum.

The difficulties facing the different churches today are thus very much alike, and they are probably insoluble if faced only within a traditional circle of assumptions about what, sociologically speaking, the church is. But do today's experimental forms of church life suggest anything better? If so, what, exactly, is the significance of their suggestion? What would it look like if generally put into practice?

Chapter IV

Toward a Polity
for Radical Ecumenism

I F THERE IS ANYTHING to be learned from these surveys, it is the crucial importance of *polity*. This word is used here to mean a great deal more than "church government." It is used to denote the way the church operates and conceives of itself as a social reality in its total political—that is to say human—environment. These relationships and concepts will have their impact on the churches' internal affairs, to be sure, but we are also concerned with the whole range of external social interactions that come into being because of what the church is and does. We are interested in the full human reality that emerges because of the intersection of the gospel with history. Polity is the posture of the church in relation to all these movements and forces in its life-world.

The purpose of any given church polity is to bring the promise of the Kingdom of God to bear upon those situations and circumstances in which men are open to humanly significant decision. Because men are social as well as individual beings, the points at which they are able to make responses truly relevant to the quality and direction of their lives will vary from one social order to another. Modern societies leave persons little room for decisions that lead to tangible changes of any kind in their personal attitudes, their social relationships and commitments, their visions of what the human world might, with man's effort, become. Instead, the "system" seems to present men with a series of nonchoices: between brands of detergents, between companies to work for, even between universities. It takes tremendous imagination in modern societies even to conceive of choices that could lead to unprogrammed ends by opening chinks, however small, in a deterministic social network.

Yet response to the gospel is supposed to entail choice of this latter kind. It is supposed to open to man the possibility of "a new heaven and a new earth." It is supposed to involve some first, tentative step in that direction. Thus it may be boldly said: the presentation of the Kingdom *must* have social implications before it has individual impact. If it does not, it confronts man with one more nonchoice. The modern listener can be pardoned if he wonders what all the fuss is about. An authentic preaching of the gospel must therefore seek out the right social location in order to be heard. It must seek out those points in the spectrum of man's thought and activity where there is openness to new commitment. These points may not be the same in the modern world as they were in the situations in which our existing church-world polities took form.

With the exception of the "free church" polities, our traditional church-world structures were built, as we have seen, "from the top down." The human possibilities to which they spoke were, for the most part, those concerned with the building of a European Christian civilization. This is true whether one thinks of the empire of Charlemagne, of the high Middle Ages, of the period of the Reformation, or of any other specific epoch. European civilization took many forms. But for many centuries and in many places the common theme was that of creating Christian cultures whose official forms and dominant institutions, whatever they were, gave social expression to faith. The relevant decision for the individual in most cases was the decision to conform. Where this was not the decision, dissent was generally aimed at creating some alternative form of Christian society, not at questioning the concept of a Christian society as such.

But now these polities, and the possibilities they sought to realize, are out of date. It is not just that we confront new forms of the old problems. The relation of man to his cultural and political achievements is now turned inside out, or upside down. In the "Constantinian" period, men could believe that the public order they maintained affirmed the human over against meaninglessness and chaos. Today, however, we are beginning to suspect that the threat of chaos comes more from the order itself than from the forces that it is intended to restrain. For the ordering of Western civilization today has become unjust, exploitative, militaristic, and in some instances, paranoid. It is an old social concept trying to maintain itself by force in a radically changed situation. The locus of human values no longer resides only in this *status quo*. It is also to be found in forces, within and without this dominant public order, that struggle against it and its values. Man fulfills himself now not only in the defense of order but also in insurgency. The meaning of this insurgency is a complex matter to which we must return. Suffice it to say now that the social location of decision for the Kingdom is different now from what it was. This difference remains to be precisely defined.

One consequence, however, is already clear. As the social location of authentic human decision changes, so does the problem of defining what the "human" really means. Ironically, the terms "human" and "humanization" have become popular in contemporary religious thought precisely at the moment when all the old definitions of such words have become inadequate. This book is a good illustration of the trend. Some, no doubt, find this highly irritating. If so, irritation may be exploited to make a point. It is *because* established patterns of society with their estab-

lished structures of thought do not tell us who man is that
the word is used so much. The very idea of man has now
become an eschatological, not a cultural, concept. We now
suspect that the genuinely human appears most often in the
revolutionary dimensions of our experience where new
possibilities come to conscious expectation, not in sectors
of our lives that are preprogrammed either by tradition or
by social management. Our ideas of the human are justly
challenged by the Black Revolution, by the rising expectations of the Third World, and by the growing conviction
of the young that their humanity, too, is left unfulfilled
by the civilization they have inherited. Thus the meaning
of the "human" remains to be worked out. The word is used
to denote the question, not the answer. To avoid the word,
as some suggest, might be to deny that the question exists.

A new polity is needed, a new vision of the humanly
relevant configuration of Christian gathering, linked to the
genuine openings to the future that exist among us and
thus to the sorts of human decision that can really be called
"conversion." The search for such a new polity will involve
far more than a rethinking of church government, far more
than ingenious construction of union plans. It will require
a reconsideration of all our theological symbols and their
meanings. It will require a search for the authentic interaction between theological symbols and human potenti-
ality.

Yet the effort to envision such a new polity reminds us
of the crisis of imagination with which this book began.
We are trying to imagine what is not yet. The traditional
habits and images are so powerful that it is difficult to think
of the church without them. The resort of apocalyptic
writers to fantastic imagery becomes more comprehensible
when one realizes what imagining a genuinely "new"
heaven and earth involves. Yet our picture will be different
from those of the Biblical visions. For one thing, it will be
better informed sociologically. The author of the Apoca-

lypse could call the great empires of the ancient world by the names of savage beasts, and make the point that man, to be truly human, needed a redemption from their clutches that only God could afford. Our search for a Christian polity today will be helped by a less mythological and more operational analysis of the predicament of modern man.

1. Man in the Modern Social Process

Man's understanding of himself is reflected in how he organizes his life in society. It is reflected in the metaphors he habitually uses in thinking and speaking about what he is doing. The "regime" he sets up shapes both his political and his religious institutions. Or, as the case may be, it provides the pattern against which he, for one reason or another, hammers out his protest. Suppose Swanson's analysis were extended to cover the contemporary situation. How might the modern social process look? What might it choose as its dominating social metaphor?

a. *The Search for a Social Metaphor*

Several contemporary writers offer clues. The Princeton sociologist Manfred Halpern has recently suggested, in effect, that the most striking feature of our contemporary situation is the *incoherence* of our life together when this is measured in human terms.[48] Halpern lists a variety of relationships between human beings fundamental to the social orders of the past and suggests that none of these relationships exists meaningfully in the advanced industrial societies of today. We do not meet. Our relationships do not cohere into community. Our meetings, instead, are external to human ways of being: they are rationalized, ideologized, computerized. The structures of social coherence that we are creating are foreign to our human natures.

Hannah Arendt argues in her book *The Human Condi-*

tion that the development of the mathematical-physical and the biological sciences has been such that it is no longer possible for scientists to use ordinary human language to describe how they believe the world works.[49] Whether this working be described in terms of abstruse formulas, a world of subatomic particles, or the interior of the cell, linguistic models drawn from ordinary experience less and less apply. This means that men cannot empathize with what they "know." They cannot *feel* how the universe is put together, or how they themselves are constructed. They cannot relate their knowledge directly either to art or to moral awareness.

In his book *The Making of the President, 1968,*[50] Theodore White writes, "The fall of 1968 could, conceivably, be the last in which an election in America is best understood by trying to understand what the leaders sought to do and tell the people." In other words, political events are now less and less in the hands of politicians, and the official political institutions and structures less and less provide the channel through which public policy decisions are actually made. The determining factors, in fact, become something of a mystery. The number of relevant "inputs" is now so large, their distortion by the communications media is so inevitable, their impact on the public is so unpredictable that people feel that human affairs are ceasing to be responsive to human will.

With such developments in mind, Stanley Kubrick's film *2001* represents both a threat and a bit of possibly illicit comfort. In *2001* a computer on a spaceship headed for Jupiter has been programmed not only with the flight plan but with a capacity for human emotions. Suspicious of the crew, it tries to take over the flight. What is this film saying? That man will be eclipsed by mechanical artifacts of his own making? Or that man will succeed in extending his human qualities into the products of his hands: that the ultimate mystery of the universe (symbolized by a giant, *manufactured* marble monolith that periodically reappears) *becomes* the mystery of man through man's success in conquering it? If computers, in fact, did behave like men, we might have a better idea of what is in store for us than we do. As it is, *2001* can be interpreted as a remarkable attempt to give human dimension to technology. The reality into which we are headed may not be so comforting.

From observations like these, in a variety of fields, contemporary man may be gradually producing a new social metaphor. It would seem that what impresses us most about our lives is the inhuman quality of the mechanisms by which decisions affecting our existence are actually reached. Such an awareness characterizes our sense of both the physicobiological and the sociopolitical worlds. It is not that we have proved, by empirical observation and logical reasoning, that our sense of ourselves as human beings has no place in these matters. It is rather that we are tempted to *assume* this and to make our metaphors accordingly. And metaphors, as we have seen, underlie the construction of social institutions, the assignment of symbols, and the evaluation of acts. They make our life-worlds what they are. They produce polity.

Swanson assigned names to the different variants of Western European polity in the Reformation period. These names were derived from typical political structures, from "centralist" to "heterarchic." Different from one another as they were, these political metaphors had in common the fact that they represented different patterns of expression of *human will*. Sometimes the society and its institutions were conceived as direct manifestations of the will of a sovereign. At other times society was thought to be generated out of conflict and compromise. But the human character of all such structures was unmistakable. The metaphors which men now tend to assign to the working of social institutions are in sharp contrast. They are metaphors from which the human quality is excluded, from which men feel alienated. If Swanson's nomenclature were extended to the present day, one might choose some such term as "cybernetic" to describe the kind of social image now coming into view.

"Cybernetics," of course, is the term invented by the mathematician Norbert Wiener to describe an approach to the world, a perspective on history, modeled on the functioning of the computer. It means more than computer science as such: it is actually a vision, a world view, that transforms everything it touches. In Wiener's hands "cybernetics" offers man powerful new tools for solving his problems. It is not an inhuman science in this sense. But man may be becoming mesmerized into using the image of the computer as a basis for his own self-understanding. If so, one of the unexpected consequences of scientific progress (about which Wiener writes humanely and eloquently in his books)[51] is already upon us. Ironic that the first unexpected consequence would not be a matter of pollution, genetic deterioration, or anything like that, but a question of the hold of an idea over men's minds!

To picture society according to a cybernetic metaphor is to assume certain things about it, to act accordingly, and therefore gradually to bring the imagined situation into actual existence. A cybernetic social system would be one in which events were conceived to be the results of a vastly complex network of impulses passing at all times in every conceivable direction between the elements in the system —in this case, human beings. Persons would have no significance apart from their roles in the system. There would be no conceivable way to get outside it. The social system would be self-directing and self-correcting, according to a program implicit in the character of the whole network, and thus beyond the control of any individual or combination of individuals within it. Even men's nervous systems would be tied into the grid. It would thus be

TOWARD A POLITY FOR RADICAL ECUMENISM 145

difficult to say where the organic left off and the electronic began. There could be no distinction between the network and its goals, no separation between the system and its symbols. The notion of transcendence, in any conceivable meaning of that word, would be out of the question.

Why should anyone want to think about society this way? There is something compulsive in this metaphor. Apart from Marshall McLuhan's imaginative warnings that "media" may be turning us into cybernetic men whether we like it or not, is there any reason why men should *choose* such an image to describe their own life-world? There are perhaps two reasons, both somewhat ironic.

First there is the nature of attempts at social *explanation* as they are carried on in contemporary social science. As students of the subject inevitably discover, sometimes to their dismay, to the extent that social science can explain how societies work and therefore can predict future social phenomena, it can also explain things about the social scientist himself and can predict the course of *his* life. Thus behind every impulse to explain social reality there is a temptation to theories of social determinism. Explanation is limited by any factor that must be considered indeterminate. If the indeterminate factor is human beings, either as individuals or in groups, this is a serious limitation for social science. Thus those who increasingly occupy the influential think-tanks and who make expensive "feasibility studies" for governments, universities, and even churches tend to popularize the assumption that society is something that makes its own rules, that man cannot get hold of it, that we are all part of a system that in the end triumphs over us.

The same conclusions are often reached, after much frustrating experience, by social managers who have tried to put new ideas into practice on a large scale. Perhaps the best example here is the field of secondary education, where the theory that integration of the races made for superior schooling has been a liberal axiom for more than a decade. The difficulty has been that quantitative measurements have by and large failed to bear this out. One can try something, and yet be unable to get hold of results. In this case, indeed, the problem may be yet deeper, for it is hard to say if integrated education has really been tried. How many school boards have made a genuine effort? How often have possible results been wiped out by dissent in the local community, by prejudice among teachers and students, or by other factors impossible to measure? In short, some of our most liberal attempts to build a better society begin to convince us that society is some kind of unfathomable mystery, and that we are in the middle of it.

In short, to believe that our large-scale social structures do have a human dimension that men can grasp begins to require an act of faith. The evidence of recent experience is against such a belief. And when such evidence is added to natural human inertia and normal human avarice, the picture is complete. For there is no more humanly alienated model of society than the one that must be in the mind of the man who opts for self-seeking privatism, or of the political cynic who opts not for progress but for power.

The privatist is the worshiper of the household idols of ancient Canaan, sure that no providence rules over history, and determined to get his share and have his comforts, even at the expense of everybody else. To him, the idea that society cannot be changed and that it is not worth trying is welcome news. Just so long as the great computer cranks out an income, he is happy. The computer put him here, and put other people there. History is inscrutable; he might as well enjoy it.

The cynical politician, on the other hand, is the worshiper of the ancient high gods, the legitimators of imperial ideologies that explain what is supposed to be happening in such a way as to keep people at each other's throats. Marxism and capitalism both fail as explanations of social process, but they do provide employment for thousands of sycophants of the gods of war and strife. Convinced that political life is in fact arbitrary, that *he* might as well get control of it if he can, the man of power convinces many by his actions that he is right.

The consequences of our modern alienation of human values from the social process are thus far-reaching and complex. To call our working metaphor cybernetic is only to suggest a word; the reality of this attitude appears in many ways. The word, indeed, could suggest just the opposite—a political community permeated by reason and responsive to leadership. The complexities of the social order, however, will not go away. Man will have to make a strenuous effort to master this fantastic system for his own good, instead of being mastered by it. To do so, he will have to invent some new kinds of humanism, adequate in their conception to the social complexities with which they must live.

Two such humanisms that deserve careful attention are now emerging. Their nature may provide clues to the kind of interactions that a modern ecumenical polity could envision. We may call them *technological humanism* and *revolutionary humanism*.[52]

b. *Technological Humanism*

Technological humanism is the faith that man's scientific intelligence, modifying the natural and social orders, can significantly improve the human condition. This is not simply to say that all scientific progress is human progress, or to assume that technological achievements will often have valuable spin-offs for the civilian market. Both things are true in their own way, but technological humanism, in the sense given this term here, means the specific intention to fight for the human cause by scientific means. Not all scientists and engineers would be willing to describe their goal in this way. For some, such an object would seem to compromise the disinterested spirit of basic research. For others, the acknowledgment of such a purpose would seem both pretentious and risky. In fact the faith which technological humanism involves is probably held by more spectators than participants in the scientific enterprise, a fact that should give us pause from the start.

Still, a somewhat naïve confidence seems to exist that science is being organized, by someone, to work in a concentrated way on human problems, and that if one waits long enough, most of the ills of mankind will therefore go away. The working scientists who take this task seriously have a much more sober view of the possibilities, especially if they often have to deal with politicians. Still, there is no doubt that technological achievements are going to modify the shape of virtually every human problem in years to come. One might as well influence this process in constructive directions if one can do so.

The technological achievements that already decisively influence the human condition hardly need mention. Many of the projects that will influence it in the future are already in view. No one needs to be convinced of the importance of these things. The question is rather that of how this tremendous enterprise can become a conscious humanism: whether, apart from the good intentions of many individuals, such a thing as technological humanism can meaningfully exist.

The basic warrant for finding a human meaning in technology lies deep in Western culture. Up to approximately the time of Galileo, technology was an instrument of existing social goals. From the temples and pyramids of ancient Mesopotamia and Egypt to the cathedrals of medieval Europe, the engineer and the craftsman were in the conscious service of the priest and the artist. The Biblical warrant is consistent with this. Man, we read in Genesis, is to subdue the earth, till the soil, name and domesticate the animals: all to make the earth a fit place for human habitation. Even Prometheus' theft of fire from the gods is not for rocketry but for the hearth. Culture defines the situation in which technology operates.

But with the sixteenth century the situation begins to change. Technological advance makes possible what we now call basic science, and the scientist makes discoveries and advances hypotheses that *themselves* define the human situation in new ways. New insights now have their impact on culture. The orthodox opinion makers find this so threatening that they try to suppress the scientist by force. But suppression cannot succeed. Science now gives man radically new perspectives on himself. It begins to mold culture instead of simply expressing it. This scientific shaping of society now works by giving man both new power (communications, transportation, medicine) and new perspectives (the earth as seen from space). It caps the process by suggesting models for human problem-solving in every realm. Most obvious are the current proposals for the extension of what amounts to engineering techniques to both the social and biological realms. If we can put men on the moon, we can use similar methods to remake man himself.

Perhaps technological humanism reaches its zenith with this last proposition, but this faith exposes its profound ambiguity at the same point. One need not dwell long on the problem of unforeseen consequences in both the social and the biological spheres. A sociological Apollo Program, if one could be put together, would no doubt require self-defeating levels of human regimentation. And as for biological engineering, unanticipated genetic results could destroy the human race instead of fulfilling it. The real problem, however, is that of social control of scientific goals, and here the conflicts that began with Galileo remain unresolved. It is not that we want still to insist that the earth is stationary and flat, or to hold any other objectively disproved proposition. It is that for science to work in the

interests of society, the whole culture must first absorb
what it will of the new definition of the human situation
that science provides, integrate this new perspective meaningfully with its humanistic tradition, and return it to the
scientist in the form of norms and goals. This, in our
present cybernetic, i.e., humanly alienated, culture is not
happening.

The more the scientist and engineer tries to formulate
a humanism, then, the more he finds himself on his own.
The more he tries to work meaningfully in and for the
human community, the more he finds it to be a noncommunity. The more he tries to derive goals from his own
professional experience, the more he finds that the scientific community, in human terms, is a noncommunity as
well. The impulse to a scientific or technological humanism
exists, but as a humanism it is incomplete. To borrow
language from theology, we could say it has no polity. It
does not successfully express itself in social interaction.
Thus it is in danger of being captured in the aimless web
of alienation, of personal privatism and public mythology,
out of which something will come but we cannot tell what.

c. *Revolutionary Humanism*

It is not surprising, therefore, that another kind of
humanism, revolutionary humanism, has surfaced in our
midst. Revolutionary humanism is the faith that man can
be fulfilled in his social nature through the radically transforming intervention of a community that is willing to
make a total break with the past. It is the faith that society
needs a "liberated zone" in which men are free from the
network of pressures that otherwise define their lives. Revolutionary communities holding this conviction today take
many forms: black, white, integrated, violent, nonviolent,
student, square, religious, secular, Marxist, Gandhian,
Buddhist, Christian, and every conceivable combination.
Such groups today differ from their sixteenth-century

counterparts in their sense of historical responsibility. They are not merely trying to live right and keep to themselves. They want to change society. In some cases they want to take it over.

One of the ironies of our cybernetic society lies in the way it has made this radical opposition to itself possible. The "system" has both limited man's imagination and made possible opportunities of education and communication that, for some, produce a radical alienation. The ideological materials for revolution have been continually present and available, but they have been embedded in the culture in such a way that most people have failed to recognize them. Now, however, this peculiar combination of repression and opportunity has produced the revolt of students in virtually every industrialized society. That an older generation, by and large, cannot understand this is evidence of the continuing power of the "system" to denature its most pregnant ideas. That others *do* grasp what is happening is a sign of strength and hope.

The roots of the revolutionary, or utopian, mentality go deep. At their origin stands Biblical eschatology, the expectation of the Messiah, the promise of the Kingdom of God. But, for the most part, Western Christian society has succeeded in managing the symbols of utopia so as to render them harmless to the establishment. In fact, utopia has often been made to work as a device for social control. The Kingdom has sometimes been so idealized and thrust so far in the future that it becomes more a justification for the troubles of the present than a challenge to them. One can bear life now if heaven comes later. On the other hand, the Kingdom has sometimes been so identified with church or society or both that talk of the imperfections of these institutions has been taboo. And even when a few men have taken the Kingdom seriously as a challenge within man's present existence, it has usually been possible to prevent them from becoming a social threat. Often they have encapsulated themselves in utopian communities. Significantly, much modern legislation in the West about religiously based social deviation, such as conscientious objection to war, has assumed that such sentiment will be relatively rare and mostly nonpolitical. Thus it has been possible to be generous. It is easy for society to make exceptions where it faces no significant challenge.

But all this has now changed. Revolutionary humanism is no longer willing to be domesticated within a situation that society has already defined. Like the technological humanism of Galileo, it pushes for a piece of the social action. It offers new perspectives on the nature of man that society cannot ignore. In this case the Galileo was Karl Marx, who grasped the element of radical eschatological expectation in the Western tradition and reformulated it in political terms. The purpose of this reformulation was not so much to destroy the theism of Christian and Jewish eschatology as to make it socially unavoidable. The theistic element, Marx realized, had become a social device for hiding the Kingdom's political and economic implications: it was opium for the people.

Not all revolutionary humanism today is Marxist, although Marxist forms of this faith are more open to dialogue with Christians than other forms of it. It would seem that students in the capitalist democracies care less about the Jewish and Christian origins of their eschatology than their counterparts in Eastern Europe! What all forms of revolutionary humanism seem to have in common, however, is the theme of radical renunciation of traditional political systems. Prevailing society, including its most liberal elements, pollutes its own best ideas with inertia and self-interest. Liberals fool only themselves. The need is for radical separation and for direct action. That way the social net is broken and human relationships become immediate. Thus it is very important for the revolutionary humanist to create not only counterforce but countercommunity. Having renounced the old forms of common life, he must prove himself capable of building and sustaining new ones.

This is the point, it must be said, at which utopian humanism has had the greatest difficulty. As soon as such a community accepts responsibility for being in the world but not of it, of transforming the world without being transformed by it, tensions difficult to surmount seem to arise. Differences of opinion quickly become tests of strength. The community divides, and often totalitarian controls, or something approaching them, are needed to keep order and continuity. The ideology of the future is overcome by the bickering of the present.

In sum, the picture of a society in which human qualities must be maintained by intellectual or political insurgency is not a happy one. The programs of insurgency themselves have too many problems. Yet the Western world is close to this situation. The human elements in the society are no longer included in the basic social model, the cybernetic system that generates both its own program and its own future. What useful interaction the church could have with such a world, apart from providing it with some legitimating and stultifying myth, is still not decided. Do the experimental Christian communities really speak to this problem?

2. Ministry in a Cybernetic Society

It could be said both of technological and of revolutionary humanists that the more seriously they take the task of opening our cybernetic culture to a human future, the more clear it becomes to them that they are isolated. The prevailing social structure is prepared to support what feeds it, but not what transcends it. In itself it is more like a complex machine than like a community. Radicals need a base of community support, rich, if possible, in profoundly human symbols of the future toward which they reach. Yet this, evidently, is something they have been able neither to create nor to find.

It is presumptuous to suggest it, but the symbols underlying the Christian Eucharist have everything to do with what these men are looking for. Presumptuous, of course, because the celebration of Communion by the churches has so seldom made this evident. The eucharistic symbols, by their very nature, are intended to make present the future of the human world. More often than not they have appeared to do the opposite: to keep alive the narrowness of the human past. We have seen that this has been, above all, a question of social location. What acts and symbols say is inseparable from their cultural and moral context.

In its original context, the Lord's Supper is without doubt a fellowship meal of revolutionaries. The symbolism of the meal likens them to guests at the great marriage feast of mankind in the Kingdom of God. This is not a mere continuation of relationships long since old and tired out. It is the future coming to meet men who are ready for it. It is an anticipation of what *will* be. Men are invited out of frustration, guilt, and futility to a table of light and joy and warmth. They come together under the sign of reconciliation to love one another. But this does not mean that they abandon the world's work. The bread and the wine point to man's ability, and duty, to cultivate the natural order with his intelligence and energy for human purposes. There is nothing magical about this transformation; it symbolizes in concentrated form what all work, scientific and otherwise, is for. The idea is to make, and keep, the world a place of healthy human habitation. There is also, of course, a reminder here of what the old world will do to men who live too resolutely in the new. Jesus' coming liquidation is graphically portrayed as the bread is broken and the wine is poured out. The future comes to meet men, but there will be strife, struggle, discouragement, failure between now and then.

The experimental communities studied in this book, along with many others, seem to be trying to place Christian faith in a context in which meanings such as these can become real. This effort has produced side effects that make the experiments difficult for some people to understand. To some extent it has alienated the experimenters from conventional Christians. It has produced forms of Christian community that last a very short time. It has involved the church with persons, movements, and ideas that seem to have little to do with Christianity as traditionally understood. But the opportunities for the church that exist today are mostly outside the precincts with which churches are most familiar. Those who are open to the future have to live "beyond." The church, if it is alive, must be there to meet them.

It is not that Christian faith, in these cases, is simply identified with future-oriented humanism. It is rather that humanisms forced to operate outside conventional structures have a perspective that the gospel seems able to illuminate, while it does not appear to speak very eloquently today to men who behave purely by custom, by rote. This, in short, is a social location in which the Biblical message seems at home. There is something of the spirit of Abraham setting forth for the Promised Land in these situations: something of Moses leading Israel out of Egypt, something of Jesus cleansing the Temple, something of young men seeing visions and old men dreaming dreams (Acts 2:17), something of John's vision of "a new heaven and a new earth" (Rev. 21:1). In such situations the gospel is being spoken where the things the gospel is about press toward realization.

Does the presence of Christian proclamation and celebration in such situations make a tangible difference? This is less easy to say with certainty. But it is not unimportant to note, first, that it makes a difference to the Christians! Most Christians involved in experimental communities seem to feel that whatever non-Christians may make of celebrations of Holy Communion in their midst, the Christians discover the concrete import of their faith in such contexts as never before. The witness of experimental communities is thus first of all to the rest of the church. These are the commitments that the church ought to be making, the causes that Christians ought to be backing, for the simple reason that these are the things the Bible again and again talks about. The human realities of liberation and reconciliation are the best classrooms for Bible study.

Beyond this, however, one can say that a ministry to the world outside the church also takes place. The whole reality with which the gospel deals is the human, not just the Christian, reality. Ministry in the midst of the world is a ministry to the profound ambiguities of every form of humanism, to the paralyzing inner contradictions of the utopian mentality. In a word, man's own capacities are not sufficient ground for the hope he often harbors in his breast. The very presence of a revolutionary hope in human experience suggests that man is in touch with powers and possibilities beyond himself. Any man who sets out upon the road of hope needs a ministry to help him deal with the pitfalls and the terrors he will meet. He needs a ministry to help him hold hoping communities together. He needs a ministry that offers him liturgical acts and symbols that bring to expression the very things he is encountering and feeling.

There is increasing evidence that experimental communities are succeeding in communicating this to people otherwise outside the church. It seems that ostensible non-Christians will participate in the reality of Communion when it is offered with no strings attached. They will acknowledge the meanings of Communion where these meanings are sufficiently indigenized. An incident indicative of this apparently took place during the Democratic National Convention in Chicago in 1968, when hundreds of protesting young people, hardly a conventionally church-going group, received the bread and wine from an Episcopal bishop in Grant Park. It would be dangerous, of course, to draw far-reaching conclusions from what must have been a highly emotional moment. But it would be foolhardy, too, to ignore what such moments could mean.

The issue, after all, is whether interpretations of the Sacrament related to social contexts long since dissolved are still sacrosanct, or whether the Sacrament really belongs to those who live its reality now. The whole fabric of Christian sacramental theology grew up in a situation in which the Western world was being Christianized from the top down. It was natural, therefore, for Communion to be fenced with legalistic restrictions and cast in metaphysical terms. But now, as Richard York of the Free Church of Berkeley likes to say, both church and society have to be "melted from the bottom up." This is bound to make a difference, the extent of which we have not yet glimpsed. Some of the implications, however, are already staring us in the face.

The Christian ministry is from freedom to freedom, from risk to risk. If such a ministry is to be credible, it must have both its social and its symbolic location fully within the ambiguous human situations to which it intrinsically speaks. Such a ministry cannot sally forth from some safe and secure social bastion and expect to be gladly received. It cannot be conceived in some situation in which man's future-yearning vulnerability is drowned in the blandishments of a vast and comforting electronic medium (whose function is to massage the conscience into sleep), and then offered to men who man the barricades. There needs to be virtually total identification between the ministry and its working context.

The witness to nonviolence, for example, is central to the Christian message. But there is a kind of "establishment pacifism"[53] that mouths the sentiment that violence is evil from a context in which violence is hardly a temptation. Such a witness will not be believed in contexts where it might count. A genuine nonviolent ministry may well have to identify itself, at the risk of misunderstanding, with movements and causes in which violence is a real and present danger. The witness against violence cannot then be mistaken for witness against the movement itself, if it is just. Such a ministry is bound to be highly contextual. It is the kind of ministry that has produced communities of the sort studied in this book.

Or consider a ministry to the world of technology, concerned with the interplay of what is possible with what is humanly responsible. How can one be sure of what is possible before it is tried, yet how can one speak of responsibility exercised only after the event? Our vastly enhanced technical possibilities make acute the question whether there are things that science *could* do which ought, for human reasons, *never* to be done. Is there ever to be an end to the principle that if a thing can be done, it will be? A ministry to the human freedom involved in such issues cannot possibly be carried out unless the minister somehow shares the possibilities and the risks himself. Again, a contextually defined ministry is the relevant kind.

Sooner or later, however, the development of experimental Christian communities and ministries will call for something like an experimental polity. This will be the real test. The existing church can try out many new ideas, but can a new kind of church be based on what such experiments have achieved? What would such a church be like? It would have to reflect the main features of the new Christian communities: their contextual nature, their adaptability, their independence of concentrations of power and wealth. It would, on the other hand, have to find ways of keeping the tradition of Biblical faith alive, of protecting this faith from distortion, and of producing theological reflection on the faith adequate to its mission. None of these requirements, in the light of past experience, should be taken lightly.

3. POLITY FOR A DIASPORA CHURCH

A number of writers of late have suggested that the roots of such an idea are already present in the Bible, in the notions of an "Exodus Church,"[54] or of a people of God in *diaspora.* The latter term, of course, means the "scattering" of both Jews and Christians in the midst of hostile environments. This was the form of existence the Hebrew people had to adopt when they were exiled to Babylon in 587 B.C. It was the situation of both Jews and Christians after the fall of Jerusalem to the Roman legions in A.D. 70, and before Constantine began to turn Christianity into a state religion in A.D. 312. A number of modern writers have explored the *diaspora* idea as a model for modern polity, among them Richard Shaull[55] and Karl Rahner.[56] The notion is both Biblical and concretely imaginable. The real question is whether, under modern conditions, it is practicable.

A social organism that has no center and no structure is not likely to survive long in the present-day world. And with the demise of the church as an organized body might well go the demise of the Biblical tradition which is the basis of the contextual ministries we have been studying. As things stand now, these experimental ministries are highly dependent on the traditional churches for theological training, for financial support, and even for a sympathetic context in which to try out new ideas. It is not true that the traditional churches are dead set against what the experimenters are trying to do. On the contrary, the new ministries are being welcomed in many quarters as openings to the future which the churches ought to follow, using whatever resources they have in the process.

There is danger, of course, for experimenters who accept the embrace of the churches too willingly. Without question, the communication of the gospel in its traditional forms is today subject to so much misunderstanding that one must come close to repudiating all that the church is thought by society to stand for before one can speak a meaningful word. Thus the experimental communities and ministries are pulled in two directions at once. There is no desire for schism. Yet there is a very great desire, and need, for freedom. The problem of polity today will have to be worked out within this tension. The problem is likely to be with us for a long time.

The difference between the old and the new in the church is not a matter of well-defined, rival theological theories. While differences of theological position do exist, the underlying factor turns out to be the different social locations in which different Christians live. A bishop, or a theologian closely connected with an official church structure, will be likely to construe the question of polity in terms of his own responsibilities, in terms of the decisions he most often must make. A pastor with activist inclinations ministering in a secularized social context will see the issue differently. A person who is more or less on the fringes of the church will have still another perspective.

The way one sees issues of theology and polity, in short, depends on the life-world within which one deals with them. Every conceivable question is included. Take, for example, the question of the meaning of "God." Christians in experimental situations use this word, it would seem, in somewhat different ways from its normal usage in traditional church contexts. Yet the difference may not be as great as the familiar differences of usage we expect from "ministers" and "laymen." The same point could be made for every other question in the theological spectrum.

The truth, of course, is that each one of us represents some combination of the old with the new, some uneasy balance between the traditional and the unknown. The so-called secular world exists not merely "out there." It is very much a part of us. The perennial problem is to work out the relationship in a way that releases creative energies instead of producing paralysis. It is thus too simple either to write off the experimental ministries as disorderly and threatening, or to write off the traditional churches as stultifying and irrelevant. To do so is to falsify the complexities *within* us: the tensions with which we inevitably have to live.

The experimental Christian communities need some kind of connectional polity. That is the logical starting point for discussion. Links between otherwise isolated congregations have been a feature of Christian existence ever since Paul began to provide them with his travels and his letters. The point of such connectionalism is a double one. The scattered churches need to share their experiences; they need the strength and visibility that connectionalism can provide. But beyond this, they need to remember their responsibility not just to their immediate involvements but to the whole of society. They need to be able to speak not just to local situations but to the larger social structures in their environment. This last point is particularly important today.

The ultimate purpose of ministering to men where the creative ambiguities of their humanity are exposed is to learn how to speak a liberating and reconciling word to the social order itself. The fact that this order today be "melted from the bottom up" instead of being ordered from the top down does not relieve the church of responsibility to care about what happens in the "system" as a whole. In other words, just as the old polities involved total interactions between church and society, so the new polity must seek out a creative form of social interaction. Otherwise, the experimental ministries will remain isolated and sectarian in character. The pitfall to be avoided is not connectionalism as such, but rather the kind of connectionalism that sets the church up as an isolated "religious" institution confronting an irreligious world, and getting nowhere in the process.

Why should today's experimental ministries not borrow the world's idea and conceive of a cybernetic polity? The point would be to build a network of communication and sharing between the humanizing encounters that take place today, a network intended to challenge and, if possible, transform the depersonalizing relationships into which men are forced by society at large. Certain concrete analogies for such a thing come quickly to mind. The civil rights and peace movements of the past decade have used just this form of organization. They have, it is true, needed a certain amount of central direction, but at their best the civil rights and peace networks have been extremely sensitive to needs felt at different points in the organism. They have avoided the authoritarian and hierarchical patterns that today falsify human relationships instead of enhancing them.

The purpose of such a polity would be to give the possibility of man's encounter with the Word of God a visibility and a structure that this possibility does not now have. The existing churches, because of the position into which they have been forced, tend to obscure the possibility. The movement now represented by all the different experiments now needs to occupy enough ground, needs to emerge as a sufficiently tangible counterforce, to give men who ought to be drawn to it something specific to join. Those who want to be part of this network should be given the opportunity. A version of Christianity different from that presented by traditional church forms needs to be publicly available. A widely held understanding of the content of Christian faith appropriate to the new kinds of human encounter needs to be worked out.

How, from a practical standpoint, might such a network

begin to appear? The answer is that such a thing is already coming into view, both within and alongside traditional church structures. A kind of connectionalism already links the various "free" churches and "liberated" communities, and there are signs that this may become much more visible in the near future. Perhaps this surfacing of the "underground" will be punctuated by a series of public eucharistic celebrations of the type that took place in Paris in the spring of 1968. If so, such acts should not be taken to represent some kind of churchly disobedience or anarchism. They could very well be forerunners of the church that is to be.

One of the factors favoring such a development is the growing similarity of the identity crises being experienced by Roman Catholic and Protestant churchmen of the left wing. Until recently, Roman Catholics have had a much more urgent identity problem than Protestants have. A revolution of rising expectations fed by Vatican II has been at the heart of this, consisting of a rediscovery of the laity by the laity themselves and an ever-increasing willingness to question hierarchical authority. The Pope has helped this along with his encyclical on birth control. So have members of the American hierarchy who tend not to recognize the Roman Catholic heroes and martyrs of the peace movement. The sense that a new kind of church must emerge is very strong here. The feeling is made still stronger by the Roman Catholic's sense of discipline, by his strong grasp of the content of tradition, by his conviction that the visible embodiment of faith is not something to be ignored.

By comparison, the Protestant identity crisis has been mild. It has, for one thing, been longer in building up. The struggles over Darwinism raised the question of authority a century ago in Protestantism, and whole generations of Protestant liberals have since assumed that the issue was resolved before *they* were born. Meanwhile Protestant church leaders have been relatively liberal on social issues. And wasn't the question of the laity settled by Luther four hundred years ago? Protestants have been weaker than Roman Catholics in the areas of tradition and discipline, and their majority, white, Anglo-Saxon status has hidden from them some of the most important things going on in society. But now there are signs that this benign situation is changing. James Forman has been a great help. For the first time Protestants are asking who should control the church and what should be done with its wealth. For the first time Protestants are leaving the church to seek more meaningful Christian lives outside.

The result is that the Protestant and Roman Catholic underground movements may now be in a position to join forces in publicly significant ways. If they do, the issue of polity will be sharply joined, because the resulting movement will clearly be outside the old church organizations, and will require a polity of its own. That polity is likely to be more like the relatively informal network already described than like any of the churches from which the movement has sprung.

One can envision, then, the emergence of an organized, but open-ended, "loyal opposition" crossing existing church lines. It will not be wholly separate from the older churches. There is little or no desire for schism. Nobody believes in the old ideology of separatism. But the new kind of Christian gathering will probably be distinct from the old. It will be much more mobile, much more willing to see the church in temporary encounters. It will replace channels of authority with channels of communication. It will be highly decentralized except at moments when the situation calls for united witness.

If such developments take place, it will be important for all concerned, traditionalists and experimentalists alike, to understand what is at stake. In the balance will be the capacity of Christianity to adapt itself, without loss of its central thrust, to conditions vastly different from those it has faced before. In the balance will be the church's ability to speak a liberating and reconciling word to a society that has lost the human touch in its basic structures and that needs to feel that touch again. The time is long past for punitive and repressive responses to innovation, although there will no doubt be some reactions of this kind. The years just ahead are crucial because they will see the new forms of faith trying to live alongside the old. The last time this happened, misunderstanding and willfulness on both sides created a schism that has lasted more than four hundred years. Now, we do not have that much time.

Notes

1. Published in Geneva by the Faith and Order Department, World Council of Churches, 1968.

2. "Beyond Intercommunion: On the Way to Communion in the Eucharist," *Study Encounter,* Vol. V (Geneva: World Council of Churches, 1969), p. 96.

3. Rodney Stark and Charles Y. Glock, "Will Ethics Be the Death of Christianity?" *Trans-Action,* June, 1968, pp. 7 ff.

4. Thomas Kuhn, *The Structure of Scientific Revolutions* (The University of Chicago Press, 1962). The writer owes this reference to a paper by Richard Shaull, "Radical Theology and Communicatio in Sacris," written for the Advisory Committee for this study.

5. J.-J. von Allmen, "Some Notes on the Lord's Supper," *Study Encounter,* Vol. II (1966), p. 54.

6. Report of the North American Task Force on the Missionary Structure of the Congregation, IV, 24, quoted by Shaull, *loc. cit.,* p. 9.

7. *Christianisme Social* is published at 20, rue de la Michodière, Paris. Quotations from other documents and periodicals in the account of the Paris Eucharist are as given in this journal and translated from the French by the writer. Additional information concerning this event was derived from an interview with Prof. André Dumas, of the French Protestant Theological Faculty in Paris.

8. As reported in *Christianisme Social,* Nos. 7–10 (1968), translated from the French by the writer.

9. Information on the events in Utrecht is based on an

article "Problems Involved in the Utrecht Universitaire Kapeldiensten," by L. A. Hodemaker and P. Tijmes, in *Wending,* October, 1962, translated from the Dutch for this study by M. Santer, and made available in manuscript form by Martin Conway.

10. The writer was present at the Athens celebration. He is also indebted to the report of this event prepared for the Advisory Committee by H. Boone Porter, to Dr. Porter's article "An Ecumenical Eucharist," *Studia Liturgica,* III, 3 (1964), pp. 180–182, and to Bishop Daniel Corrigan's article "New Year's Eve at Athens," *The Living Church,* April 26, 1964.

11. Copies of the Basel papers as well as a volume-length report of the meeting entitled *A Challenge to the European University* can be obtained from the Office of the WSCF, 13 Rue Calvin, Geneva, Switzerland.

12. The account of the Arlington Heights service is based on a case study written for the Advisory Committee by Paul Chapman. Quotations are as given in this source.

13. Information on the Medellin event is based on *Christianisme Social,* Nos. 7–10 (1968), Quotations as given in this source are translated from the French by the writer.

14. Malcolm Boyd, in "The Underground Church," *Commonweal,* April 12, 1968, p. 97.

15. Rocco Caporale, S.J., "Underground and Group Churches," an address given at the Boston College Institute on the Underground Church, April 19–21, 1968.

16. Theodore M. Steeman, "The Underground Church: The Forms and Dynamics of Change in Contemporary Catholicism," in *The Religious Situation, 1969,* ed. by Donald R. Cutler (Beacon Press, Inc., 1969), p. 715.

17. *Ibid.,* p. 713.

18. *Ibid.,* p. 720.

19. *Ibid.,* p. 745.

20. Information on the Free Church of Berkeley is based on Robert A. McKenzie, "The 'Free' Church of Berkeley's Hippies" and Elsie Thomas Culver, "The Hippies' Pastor Is Ordained," both in *The Christian Century,* April 10, 1968. Data brought up to date in an interview with Richard York, July, 1969. Quotations are as given in these sources. See also John

Pairman Brown, *The Liberated Zone* (John Knox Press, 1969).

21. Information on Emmaus House is based on its periodical *The Bread Is Rising;* additional data is in Francine du Plessix Gray, "The Bread Is Rising," *The New Yorker,* Jan. 25, 1969. Quotations are as given in the latter source.

22. Ecumenical Commission, Archdiocese of Boston, *In Search of Unity: Supplementary Interim Guidelines for Ecumenical Activity in the Archdiocese of Boston,* May, 1969, pp. 7 f.

23. A survey of the present situation can be found in "Marriage and the Division Among the Churches," *Study Encounter,* Vol. III (1967).

24. Ecumenical Commission, Archdiocese of Boston, *op. cit.,* p. 8.

25. Account in *Christianisme Social,* Nos. 7–10 (1968), pp. 471 f.

26. Text of the provisional directive of the Dutch bishops quoted in English in *One in Christ,* No. 3 (1968), p. 312.

27. Ecumenical Commission, Archdiocese of Boston, *op. cit.,* p. 9.

28. Quoted in *One in Christ,* No. 3 (1968), p. 319.

29. Guy E. Swanson, *Religion and Regime* (University of Michigan Press, 1967).

30. The text is supplied by Orthodox authorities and reproduced in *Inter-Church Communion Survey,* compiled by Richard Johnson for the Advisory Committee.

31. English translation in *Diakonia,* Vol. 2, No. 2 (1967), p. 179.

32. *Ibid.,* pp. 183 ff.

33. For a detailed discussion of the history and current Orthodox views of the meaning of "economy," see F. J. Thomson, "Economy," *The Journal of Theological Studies,* N.S., Vol. XVI, Pt. 2 (1965).

34. The historical account is based on a paper "Communicatio in Sacris: Post-Trent Developments in Roman Catholic Canonical Legislation," prepared for the Advisory Committee by Father Charles von Euw. See also Wilhelm de Vries, S.J., "Communicatio in Sacris," *Concilium,* Vol. 4

(Paulist Press, 1965), pp. 18 ff.; Maurice Bevenot, S.J., "Communicatio in Sacris" in *Christian Unity: A Catholic View,* ed. by John C. Heenan (Sheed & Ward, Inc., 1962); Bernard Leeming, S.J., *The Vatican Council and Christian Unity* (London: Darton, Longman & Todd, Ltd., 1966).

35. English translation in *The Documents of Vatican II,* ed. by Walter M. Abbott, S.J. (Guild Press, Inc., The America Press, Association Press, 1966), 341 ff.

36. *Decree on Ecumenism,* Ch. 2., par. 8.

37. *Ibid.,* Ch. 3, par. 15.

38. *Ibid.,* Ch. 3, par. 22.

39. *Directory,* United States Catholic Conference, May 14, 1967, par. 55.

40. In "Liturgy and Unity," *The Ecumenist,* Vol. 6, No. 1 (Nov.-Dec., 1967), pp. 97 ff.

41. For a detailed account and copious bibliography, see N. Sykes, *The Church of England and Non-Episcopal Churches in the Sixteenth and Seventeenth Centuries* (London: S.P.C.K., 1949).

42. For more detail, see John Findlow, "Restricted Communicatio in Sacris Between Anglicans and Romans," a working paper of the Joint Working Group of the World Council of Churches and the Roman Catholic Church (Geneva, 1965).

43. Quoted in *Intercommunion Today* (London: Church Information Office, 1968), p. 160. Quotations from other documents are as given in this source.

44. *Ibid.,* p. 149.

45. *Ibid.,* p. 65.

46. This and other documents are as quoted in Vilmos Vajta (ed.), *Church in Fellowship* (Augsburg Publishing House, 1963).

47. Marcel Pradervand (ed.), *Proceedings of the 17th General Council* (Geneva: The World Alliance of Reformed Churches, 1954).

48. Manfred Halpern, "Conflict, Violence, and the Dialectics of Modernization," a paper presented to the 64th Annual Meeting of the American Political Science Association, Washington, D.C., Sept. 6, 1968.

49. Hannah Arendt, *The Human Condition* (Doubleday & Company, Inc., 1959), p. 3.

50. Theodore White, *The Making of the President, 1968* (Atheneum Publishers, 1969), as quoted by Bill Moyers, "The Election in the Year of Decay," *Saturday Review,* Aug. 9, 1969, p. 53.

51. See, for example, Norbert Wiener, *God and Golem, Inc.* (The MIT Press, 1964).

52. I owe this terminology to a conversation with Charles West in September, 1967. I have since learned that Professor West developed the typology of technological and revolutionary humanism in a paper, "Technologists and Revolutionaries," delivered at the American Society of Christian Ethics in January, 1967, and that he carries the topic considerably farther in a book, *The Power to Be Human: Toward a Secular Theology,* due to be published by The Macmillan Company in the summer of 1970.

53. The concept is John Pairman Brown's. See his book *The Liberated Zone.*

54. This is the title of the final chapter of Jürgen Moltmann's *Theology of Hope* (Harper & Row, Publishers, Inc., 1967).

55. See Richard Shaull, "The Form of the Church in the Modern Diaspora," *The Princeton Seminary Bulletin,* Vol. LVII, No. 3 (March, 1964), pp. 3 ff.

56. See Karl Rahner, *The Christian Commitment,* tr. by Cecily Hastings (Sheed & Ward, Inc., 1963).